IRELAND

MAX CAULFIELD

PHOTOGRAPHY BY JOE CORNISH

GILL & MACMILLAN

AUTHOR'S DEDICATION
For Mary Mitchell McCoy

PHOTOGRAPHER'S DEDICATION
*The photographs are for Chloe, who in mind, within
and in person travelled with Jenny and me on our
journeys in this land of sunshine and rain.*

The publishers gratefully acknowledge the assistance of
Colin Maddock at Kershaws, 501 Cotton Exchange, Old Hall St,
Liverpool L3 9LD, with travel arrangements.

HALF-TITLE PAGE *Geometric rock formations at the
Giant's Causeway, Co. Antrim.*
OPPOSITE TITLE PAGE *The tranquil waters of Lough Erne,
Co. Fermanagh, offer exceptional fishing.*

Text © Max Caulfield 1993
Photographs © Joe Cornish 1993
Maps © George Philip 1993

First published in 1993 by George Philip, an imprint of
Reed Books, 81 Fulham Road, London SW3 6RB
and Auckland, Melbourne, Singapore and Toronto.
First published in Ireland in 1993 by Gill & Macmillan,
Goldenbridge, Dublin 8 with associated companies
throughout the world.
This paperback edition 1997

ISBN 0 7171 2536 X

Produced by Mandarin Offset
Printed in Hong Kong

Contents

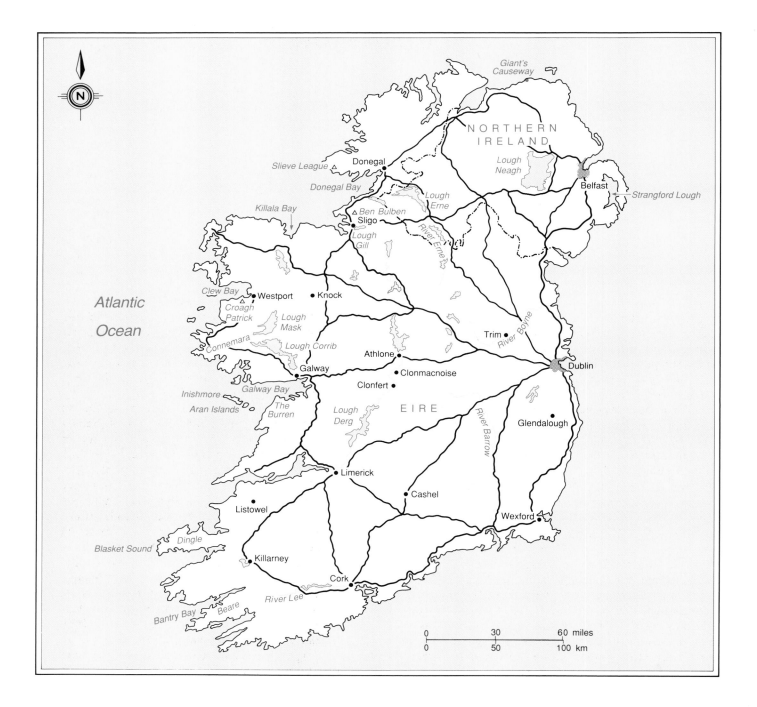

Introduction

Half the magic of Ireland lies in the people themselves, for whom splendid talk and high good humour are the very wine and stuff of life. Yet the landscape itself is heart-melting and unforgettable. Set amid the uncertainties of Atlantic weather, with cold green sea lashing its beautiful shores, the island of Ireland has been lavishly compensated by nature for its isolated position as the last outpost of Europe.

Warmed by the Gulf Stream, which encourages sub-tropical plants and flowers in its southern counties, it enjoys a temperate climate, with its main enchantments lying along a majestic coastline. The entire western seaboard, in particular, is a scenario of high geological drama. In the extreme south-west there are no fewer than four magnificent mountainous peninsulas, the most spectacular being Beare and Dingle. All are embayed by deeply penetrating sea-loughs, one of which, Bantry Bay, occupies its own special niche in Irish history because it was here in 1796 that a French revolutionary fleet, which might have altered the fate of Britain, vainly rode at anchor, waiting for storms to abate. To the north, in Co. Clare, is a strange interval of striated limestone ridges which mystifyingly change colour according to the light, making up the bizarre, if unexpectedly lovely, lunarscape of the Burren. There are other great bays, such as Donegal and Clew, vast enough to have fooled Armada captains into believing that they had reached the safety of the open Atlantic, and roaring channels such as Blasket Sound where their ships were ripped open by the rocks.

There are myriad scatterings of intriguing islands such as Inishmore in the Aran islands, which houses an enigmatic Celtic fortress called Dun Aengus, one of the finest prehistoric monuments in Europe, perched dizzyingly like a half coin on the very edge of a 300-foot cliff. Or Skellig Michael, a mere sheaf of rocky pinnacles where, in incredibly cramped beehive stone huts, monks in the Dark Ages prayed for the souls of pagan Europe. There is an *embarras du choix* of deserted beaches, pale yellow in colour and hemmed by rocks and mollusc-laden pools, and wide-spreading, seemingly endless estuaries such as Killala, where a French army *did* land in 1798 to succour an Irish rebellion which, ironically, had already collapsed. There are Europe's most magnificent sea cliffs, rising to 2000 feet at Achill Island, off Co. Mayo, and, at Slieve League in Co. Donegal, detritus of quartzite beds laid down by ancient Caledonian folding. With

colonies of whirling seabirds, indented coves and islets, it is a coastline where the traveller will undoubtedly be compelled to linger a while to drink in the magnificence of nature and breathe the very purest of air while, perhaps, staring hypnotized at the tremendous spectacle of the Atlantic. And where, eventually, someone is bound to sidle up and, with his tongue only half in his cheek, tell you that out there – and he has seen it himself – lies Hy-Brasil, the Isle of the Blest (Columbus accepted the legend), and furthermore, that if you climb that nearby mountain you will be able to see people walking in the streets of New York. Ireland, I should warn, does a splendid trade in the commerce of the imagination.

At this point a douche of frankness is, perhaps, called for. The face of Ireland, apart from its often ravishing landscape and the intermittent charms of what is left of Georgian Dublin, the cities of Cork and Kilkenny and Viking settlements such as Wexford and Waterford, may sometimes appear drab and depressing to you. A number of Irish towns and villages are, at best, as nondescript as a huddle of shacks on the American prairies. There are, fortunately, ample exceptions, particularly in the east and south, and one can stumble across beautiful little places like Inistioge on the River Nore in Co. Kilkenny, which has a ten-arched eighteenth-century bridge, a square with lime trees and the remains of a thirteenth-century Augustinian friary, but as a general rule, the further west you travel, the less captivating the villages. Here and there, too, the traveller will become aware of scabrous and derelict cottages with blind windows, and be reminded of the pervasive poverty that stalked much of this land not more than two generations ago. One should not visit Ireland looking for architectural glories comparable with Versailles or Santa Maria Maggiore, or worthy to stand alongside Chartres or the whipped-

Kilkenny City at dusk. This winding huddle of small houses overlies a Norman town plan, and is typical of the humdrum nature of most small Irish towns.

cream extravagances of Wurzburg; nor is there anything to approach the quiet, mellow, English village beauty of Lower Slaughter or Chipping Camden. This is a countryside with a rural economy engaged in a constant struggle for survival, and, although it bears many of man's traces stretching back to a time before Egypt ever crowned a pharaoh, it has never raised a great urban culture, the prerequisite of high architecture. And yet, aside from landscape, it has much to offer; it is littered with the most extraordinary remains, historic and prehistoric, secular and religious, pagan and Christian, that are likely to be found anywhere within such a small compass. And everything is bound up with the mythology of old gods and champions that echo the Homeric world, with Christian saints and holy men, with murderous Norman

The cliffs of Achill Island, Co. Mayo, viewed from Atlantic Drive. With its fine beaches and precipices of 2000 ft, the island affords exhilarating walks.

9

knights and with proud and defiant Gaelic chieftains battling for lost causes. There are the footprints of Elizabethans such as Raleigh and Spenser, of Cromwell, of Jacobites and William of Orange, of radical heroes such as Wolfe Tone and Robert Emmet – whose magnificent peroration to his speech from the dock was to prove an inspiration to nationally-minded Irishmen for over a hundred years – or of Charles Stewart Parnell, that most charismatic and unfortunate of Victorian parliamentarians. Ireland, someone once said, 'is a minor country with a major history'.

To begin with, there are over forty thousand dolmens, wedge-shaped passage graves and ring forts, including the four-thousand-year-old sacral site of legendary Tara itself, that record the passing of Stone Age, Neolithic and Bronze Age man; there are also numerous hill-forts, such as the Grianan of Aileach in Co. Donegal and Staigue Fort in Kerry which, together with standing Ogham stones incised with runic markings and other artefacts, reflect the culture of the Iron Age. The whole collection together spans some six to eight thousand years of history in a manner not replicated elsewhere. Crowning it are the magnificent quasi-religious prehistoric sites at Brugh-na-Boinne (Newgrange) and others nearby along the River Boyne, which for centuries were the burial places of the kings of Tara and which pre-date Stonehenge by a millennium, pre-date the pyramids, pre-date the first use of pictographic script by the Sumerians and even pre-date, if not the first city states of the Near East, at least the first great empires there. Brugh-na-Boinne stood when Babylon first raised its hanging gardens.

It is worth noting, perhaps, that Ireland's earliest name, known to us from Himilco, a Phoenician sailor who travelled here in the fifth century BC, was Sacra or the Sacred Island. Then, from the sixth to the tenth century AD, Ireland became the dynamo of Western Christianity as barbarian hordes drowned out what was left of the classical empire. Known as the *peregrini* (or 'wanderers for Christ'), they left their traces from the Irish Sea to the Adriatic, founding great schools and monasteries, teaching and debating, providing philosophers and men learned in Latin and Greek at a time when even emperors could not read, and eventually earning their tiny country, by then the most civilized in the West, its magnificent title 'The Isle of Saints and Scholars'. (The vitality of their missionary zeal is still proclaimed today by the presence of many Irish priests, nuns and teachers working throughout both the developed and undeveloped worlds.) Religious fervour in Ireland may no longer be what it was, nor are the edicts of the Catholic hierarchy listened to with the same respect, but crowds still attend mass on Sundays and one marvels at the spectacle of stoic piety still exhibited by the penitential pilgrims to St Patrick's Purgatory in Lough Derg or those who, sometimes bare-footed, make the ascent of Croagh Patrick, the 'holy mountain' in Co. Mayo. A pilgrimage to Knock in Mayo, where – it is believed by many – there was a vision of the Virgin in 1879, attracts hundreds of thousands every summer, and 'unexplainable' cures are alleged to have been effected there. All over the country this enduring interest in religion can be seen, even in the most unlikely forms. Near Ballyvourney in Co. Cork there is a slab of stone covered with bizarre votive offerings to St Gobnait, a local saint; everywhere there are holy wells which have become places of local pilgrimage, where votive offerings are displayed and where the pagan habit of tying bits of cloth on to a bush, or dropping pebbles into the well as a prayer is offered up, still continues in a land which has been Christian for sixteen hundred years.

The ancient Celts of Ireland regarded the other world as almost tangible and perceptible. They even 'humanized' a whole race of supernatural beings – the Tuatha de Danaan or 'peoples of the goddess Danu' – whom they envisaged as powerful magicians who had once ruled Ireland and whom they had to overcome in battle. Following defeat and using magic arts, the

Carrowmore Megalithic Cemetery, Co. Sligo, is, apart from Carnac in Brittany, the largest concentration of Bronze Age chambered tombs in Europe.

Danaans threw a veil of invisibility over themselves and became masters of the unseen, vanishing into those great mounds and raths, or ring forts, that still dot the Irish countryside. Here, within fairy palaces, they still live in Tir-na-nÓg, the Land of Youth, emerging from time to time as a leprechaun or perhaps a banshee (*bean sí*, 'woman of the fairies') whose appearance foretells disaster. The Irish, possibly because their druidic religion already taught the doctrine of the soul's immortality, had little difficulty accepting Christianity, and their new-found fervour survived because Ireland escaped barbarian invasion at a time when the old Western Roman Empire was disintegrating. The island may have no great Gothic cathedrals comparable with Nôtre Dame, Cologne, Rheims or Salisbury (Christ Church in Dublin is a Viking foundation and St Patrick's is Norman, if much restored) but it has an impressive legacy of buildings from earlier ages not easily matched elsewhere: the ruins of tiny, gem-like churches and oratories such as the sixth-century St Kevin's in Glendalough, Co. Wicklow; St Brendan's at Clonfert, Co. Galway, also sixth-century, which has a glorious Hiberno-romanesque doorway; or the remarkable eighth-century unmortared-stone Gallarus Oratory at Ballynana in Co. Kerry.

I can think of nowhere else in northern Europe that so prodigally reflects a period of history when most of the region, including Britain, lay in turmoil. Among the most evocative of ruins is that of sixth-century Clonmacnoise, on the east bank of the River Shannon near Athlone. Among the earliest Western proto-universities, it now displays the wreckage induced not only by philistine time and by the efforts to raze it of the Norse king, Turgesius (who for his pains was later drowned in a lake by King Malachy I), but also by the cannon balls of Cromwell. Nowhere else, either, can

The west door of Clonfert Cathedral, Co. Galway, with its six orders of arches and riot of decoration, is one of the high points of Irish romanesque.

one see so many round towers, one hundred and twenty of them in all, the tallest soaring 108 feet; they began their lives as peaceful monastic bell-towers or *campanili* from which the faithful could be called to prayer but ended up as wellnigh impregnable fortresses for monks and their precious treasures – golden vessels, reliquaries and illuminated manuscripts – when the Vikings descended on Ireland, wrecking and destroying. There are astonishing high crosses carved with biblical scenes, which along with the superb metalwork of the Ardagh Chalice and the Cross of Cong, as well as the exquisite illuminations of the Book of Durrow and the Book of Kells (said to be the 'most beautiful book in the world') epitomize standards of artistry stretching back to traditions smothered elsewhere in Europe by the Romans. Françoise Henry, in her book *Early Christian Irish Art*, emphasizes that 'Irish art . . . stands out as the most satisfying and most perfect form of non-representational art which Europe has ever known'. The contours of mind and imagination that produced this art carried on into the Merovingian and Carolingian periods and provided a matrix for romanesque sculpture.

The Irish landscape was to be further enriched following the twelfth-century Norman invasion and the envelopment of the isolated Irish Church by the Church of Rome. The Normans threw up massive stone castles, hitherto unknown in Ireland, by which they reinforced the power they had won with spear and battle-axe; these ruins, particularly the massive remains of Hugh de Lacy's castle at Trim, Co. Meath, where several Irish parliaments were held in medieval times, still inspire awe. Rome brought something more mellow, Cistercian and Augustinian abbeys and friaries whose ruins now stand in sombre majesty: Mellifont in the Boyne Valley, Jerpoint Abbey in Co. Kilkenny, massive, brooding Dunbrody Abbey, Co. Wexford, built by the seneschal to Strongbow himself, leader of the Norman invaders – and many others.

By the eighteenth century, large parts of Ireland had blossomed into a kind of reflection of their wealthy and dominating neighbour, England. A poor reflection, of course, for the Irish countryside, then as now almost exclusively pastoral and not farmed to the advanced standards common in England, had only a wild, rough image to set alongside the smooth patina and manicured trim of the then richest country on earth. Nor did the life of Irish peasants in the remotest way reflect the world of their counterparts in Britain. Catholic Ireland was a conquered country and the Irish had learned to touch their caps and hide their feelings, or to create caricatures of themselves full of whimsy that charmed, rather than alarmed, their masters. Yet even while the indigenous Irish multiplied furiously, scrabbled for dear life (famine and starvation were endemic) on smaller and smaller patches of land for which they paid higher and higher rents, a splendid new Ireland was already rising. Georgian Dublin gradually took shape; great Palladian and neo-classical mansions such as Castletown (built by William Conolly, Speaker of the Irish Parliament and the country's first millionaire) and Carton (seat of the dukes of Leinster), both in Co. Kildare, and Castle Coole, in Co. Fermanagh, began to give Ireland a veneer comparable with other parts of Europe.

By the start of the twentieth century, there were more than two thousand such magnificent houses throughout Ireland, with wide estates and thousands of tenants. Owned by a caste called the Ascendancy, largely, though not by any means all, Protestant and of English descent, they produced such great names as Wellington and Berkeley (the philosopher after whom the campus at the University of California is named). They were, in general, educated and cultivated although far too many were arrogant, reckless and spendthrift and spent too little time on their estates, preferring the delights of London and Bath. In 1843 the third Earl of Rosse, of Birr Castle, Co. Offaly, built a telescope that was then the largest in the world (it remained so for seventy-five years), and his son was the first man to measure accurately the heat of the sun and survey the spiral nebulae.

Among the superb legacies left to modern Ireland by the Ascendancy are a series of gardens that can stand comparison with England's greatest – among them the magnificent gardens and waterfall at Powerscourt in Co. Wicklow, Mount Usher gardens at Ashford, also in Wicklow, the demesne of Johnstown Castle, Co. Wexford, and the gardens at Beaufort, Killarney; in Northern Ireland those at Mount Stewart on the shores of Strangford Lough, formerly the seat of the Marquess of Londonderry, are among the finest in the British Isles. Because of Ireland's moist, benign climate, plants gathered from all over the world grow easily and luxuriantly – rhododendrons and blue poppies from the Himalayas, wood lilies and bloodroot from America, tree ferns and giant Chatham Island forget-me-not from New Zealand.

Leaving aside the western coastline, which is famous for its beauty, Ireland is rich in lovely countryside, even around its great industrial centres: the city of Belfast, capital of Northern Ireland, sits at the head of a magnificent sea lough surrounded by hills and mountains, with the fabled Mountains of Mourne within view of Belfast Castle. Dublin, capital of the Republic and for centuries the centre of English power in Ireland, has its own splendid beaches, Dollymount and Sandymount Strands, and, just a short distance to the south, Killiney Bay, which has been called the Irish Bay of Naples. For lush countryside with rich and fertile fields, most of the east coast would fit in neatly enough with one's idea of English landscape, but although much of Wicklow, for instance, has a soft and wistful air, it also has expanses of moorland only slightly less wild and fierce-looking than Scotland's Rannoch Moor; several peaks rise to over 2000 feet and Lugnaquilla, at over 3000 feet, is Ireland's third highest mountain. Further south the scenery is rich and bosky, with long stretches of roadway passing under the arched branches of trees; yet the savage old Ireland is always there, its bumpy prominences and mountain chains, even if dipped below the horizon, reminding one of its presence.

The Burren, Co. Clare. A 325-square-mile region which looks like a sea of grey pumice, it is softened only by the rare plants growing in its rocky fissures.

Of course, no part of Ireland truly looks like Surrey for there is always an element of wildness here, of a landscape not quite tamed. In the Republic, in any case, houses, shops, gardens, names, all look different. The signposts too, couched in prominent Gaelic with the English equivalent spelled out underneath, but never, it would seem to non-Irish eyes, with quite the same prominence, remind British visitors that they are indeed abroad. The telephone boxes, labelled 'Telefón' in Irish script, the use of Gaelic over the doors of Post Offices and other state institutions and its liberal use on official documents, confirm that the Republic's official language is not English but Gaelic, an ancient tongue with similarities to the Sanskrit spoken by the Aryans who subjugated the dark peoples of India two thousand years ago. One hundred and fifty years ago this language, as it had been from the fourth century AD, was the Irish vernacular; today nearly everyone speaks a smattering of it but it is still the mother tongue only in remote areas known as the Gaelteacht.

Irish roads too have a character of their own. The Romans with their straight roads never got to Ireland, despite the opinion of Agricola, Governor of Britain, that he would need only one legion to conquer it (paradoxically, while the Irish have felt insulted by this slur, they also have a sense of deprivation because conquest by Rome would have given them an urban fabric which they failed to develop on their own). Although 'N' roads, or national roads, linking all the major centres, are invariably wide and well-surfaced (though nowadays cars and, worse, juggernauts are destroying that quality of peace and quiet which Ireland had, uniquely, to offer), secondary roads tend to meander alarmingly as they follow the contours of the country. It is quite practicable, if highly inadvisable, to drive round all Ireland in a single day. Travellers have always complained that Irish miles are insufferably long ('Ah, but they're very *narrow*' is the classic Irish riposte), but it is a fact that a journey of forty miles in the remoter parts of Ireland can seem like eighty to a hundred elsewhere. Nor do signposts always help; it is not uncommon to encounter two set up within yards of each other, one of which says that Ballymuck, for instance, is ten miles away and the other that it is twelve. In Listowel, in Co. Kerry, there are (or were) two signposts pointing in diametrically opposite directions to the same place.

Still travelling south, one sails past the great Leinster chain of mountains, over seventy miles long, to the Golden Vale which stretches into the distance from the Rock of Cashel, ancient seat of the kings of Munster, a noble panorama bounded by the blue peaks of the Galtees and Knockmealdown. On into Cork, the largest county, offering another bewildering variety of landscape, and then, as though drawn by a magnet, into West Cork and the beginning of that superb West I have already spoken of, which runs three hundred miles away northwards to the very tip of Donegal. And this is quickly a different world. Quiet, civilized scenery begins to fall away. The mountainous, panoramic world of Kerry with, at its core, sweet Killarney and echoes of Victorian sentimentality, rise up nobly to confront you. Then, very rapidly, you are into regions where you wonder how men ever found subsistence. This is Connacht, a poor, desolate, wild, rocky yet intensely picturesque country which has to take the Atlantic elements on the chin; it was here that Cromwell, after he had smashed Catholic Ireland and seized two-and-a-half million acres, ordered Norman and Gael alike, if they were Papist, to get to 'Hell or Connacht!' Enormous rocks strew the ground everywhere; fields are no longer enclosed by untamed hedges but defined by walls of unmortared stone as if in the wilds of Anatolia; in some places these fields have no gates – when an opening is needed a gap is created simply by pulling the loose stones away.

Mayo is mountain, moorland and bogland. For centuries, in the absence of coal, the bogs of Ireland have provided the rural population with fuel; they simply dug up sods of turf (known elsewhere as peat),

Benbulben, Co. Sligo, seen from Rosses Point. In the shadow of the frontal bluffs, Ireland's greatest poet, W. B. Yeats, lies buried in Drumcliff churchyard.

stacked them to dry and then burned them in open hearths, the glorious scent wafting into the air and filling the countryside with a delicious incense. Now, however, where hardly a decade ago men laboured, digging the turf by hand, machinery performs the task more rapidly, and most farmers buy neatly-packaged briquettes which seem to me to be devoid of scent.

Mayo surrenders the ground to Sligo, famed for its table-topped limestone summit of 'bare Ben Bulben', a storied county even if the poet Yeats, who is buried in the mountain's shadow, had never lived. Here the legend of the lovers, Dermot of the Love Spot and Grania, had its dark climax: having run away together the night before she was due to marry Finn MacCool, the great but ageing Celtic champion, they were pursued all over Ireland for sixteen long years, sleeping wherever they could; finally, tricked into ascending Ben Bulben by the vengeful Finn, Dermot was forced to face an enchanted boar, which had already slain thirty men that morning, and met a terrible fate. Not far away is the site of 'The Battle of the Books', fought between the followers of St Columba and those of St Finnian of Moville. Columba had copied a psalter of Finnian's and the latter appealed to the high king on the grounds of infringement of copyright (or its sixth-century equivalent) and demanded the copy. 'As to every cow its calf, so to every book its copy', adjudicated the king. Columba, destined to become one of the greatest of Irishmen, refused to accept the ruling and, in the ensuing battle, over three thousand of his opponents were slain. For a penance, Columba exiled himself from Ireland and in 563 AD founded his famous monastery on the Hebridean island of Iona. All, indeed, is fabled land around here. Nearby is the 1000-foot hill of Knocknarea ('the hill of the kings'), topped by an enormous cairn raised over what is reputed to be the grave of Queen Maeve of Connacht, chief protagonist of the warrior hero Cuchulainn in that greatest of Celtic epic poems *The Cattle Raid of Cooley*.

And then one is into wild, highland Donegal – the misty rain still cloaking Yeats's visionary Hosts of the Shee – with its real roaming herds of red deer and its romantic memories of the young chieftain Red Hugh O'Donnell who made the last strike for Gaelic Ireland in Elizabethan times; he left behind the shell of his impressive castle which still overhangs Donegal Town, having burned it down himself to prevent its use by the English. The marvellous beaches of the far north-west, some of which seem to go on forever, link the Republic to Northern Ireland, which has a fine coastline of its own, and here the Western Isles of Scotland loom so near it appears you could touch them.

Ireland may be physically disjoined from Europe – it was cut off some nine thousand years ago, leaving it without poisonous snakes but also, alas, without nightingales, not to mention dormice, common and water shrews, moles, voles, weasels, polecats and tawny owls, and with a range of vegetation only three-fifths the extent of Britain's – but it has shared in its convulsions. The Tertiary disturbances that produced the Alps also inaugurated the volcanic activity that formed the basalt plateau of Antrim, and with it the Giant's Causeway, an improbable conglomerate of hexagonal columns that look as if they had been chiselled by Irish cousins of Hercules. Mendelssohn, having seen similar formations on the Scottish side of the North Channel, was inspired to write his overture *Fingal's Cave*; Dr Johnson, on the other hand, dismissed Antrim's much more impressive example of nature's grotesquerie as 'Worth seeing, but not worth going to see', a reaction fostered possibly by the lack of package-tours in the eighteenth century. In my view, the Giant's Causeway is worth going to see in the same way that it is worth travelling to New York to see its skyline; neither of them is altogether believable.

When the time comes for you to leave Ireland, you may well be caught up in a tangle of contrary impressions, some, no doubt, created by the extraordinary theatre of the Irish themselves and their well-known love of language. You will perhaps have prepared yourself for this, and although you may not be aware that skill with words was as highly prized in ancient Ireland as was the skill of the warrior, or that poets, in particular, enjoyed a special status in society, you will almost certainly know that the English language has been adorned for centuries by men associated with Ireland: Spenser wrote his *Faerie Queene* here; Congreve was schooled in Ireland, as was Farquhar; Sterne was born in Clonmel, where Trollope later began writing novels. Beginning with Jonathan Swift, whose epitaph in St Patrick's Cathedral begins:

Here lies the body of Jonathan Swift, DD,
Dean of this cathedral,
where savage indignation can
lacerate his heart no more . . . ,

the roll-call of great poets, novelists and dramatists cannot really be matched anywhere else in proportion to population: it includes names such as Sheridan, Goldsmith, Thomas Moore, Oscar Wilde, Bernard Shaw, Yeats, Synge, James Joyce, Sean O'Casey, Samuel Beckett and, peeking over everybody's shoulder, that mischievous imp and comic genius Flann O'Brien. You may want to see a play at the Abbey Theatre, Dublin, whose influence on literary Ireland has been immense; you will, indeed, find theatre flourishing all over the country, with special groups in places like Galway and Londonderry (whose Brian Friel is celebrated both in London and on Broadway). You will probably discover for yourself recently-dead poets such as Patrick Kavanagh or very-much-alive Seamus Heaney.

Irish wit and fantasy seem to bear no relation to the dark, cruel history of the country, to the awful poverty and suffering that saw the population drop by at least a quarter following the Great Famine of the 1840s, when blight again struck the potato crop (the staple diet of the poorest in ireland), or that made the Dublin slums, even as late as 1920, the worst in Europe, worse even than Naples. Irish history deserves a Goya (I vividly recall seeing Elizabethan woodcuts of soldiers returning triumphantly from a foray bearing the hapless, blood-dripping heads of Irish peasants upon their swords). Nor is the landscape a true reflection of the grimness of Ireland's past. One of my own dominating impressions of the land is of its colours and light, of its infinite shades of green, of course, and of a blue – almost a Venetian blue – from

A shop-front in Dingle, Co. Kerry. Vivid colours are often used to brighten up an otherwise featureless façade.

Titian or Tiepolo in its great hump-backed mountains, with a commingling of browns and mauves in bogs and moorland; a country best portrayed in watercolours, not in oils like Landseer's Scotland. (Almost equally memorable are the chocolate brown of its national drink, stout, and the amber of its greatest invention, whiskey or *uisce beatha*, meaning 'water of life', the parent of all similar distillations such as Scotch and Bourbon.)

You might also share my second impression which is of space – of a panoramic scale that defies the logical limits of such a small island. The reason for this phenomenon is that over most of the country there is little to obscure your view of the horizon, since major towns are few and far between. In terms of population density, Ireland is a crazily lop-sided country, with most people clustering along the eastern seaboard

(Belfast and Dublin alone accommodate a third of their state populations).

The division of Ireland into two political entities as a result of the Anglo-Irish Treaty of 1921 – a sovereign state administering twenty-six of Ireland's thirty-two counties, Northern Ireland the rest – may appear whimsical to a visitor only sketchily aware of the country's history. The incongruity dissolves rapidly when, on arrival from the South, you first hear harsh Northern accents which have more in common with Glasgow than Dublin, and see nailed up on wayside trees placards which, in place of the ubiquitous Marian shrines· of the South, boldy admonish you that 'The Wages of Sin is Death' or announce that 'Jesus Saves', alerting you to the fact that you have stepped outside the limits of the Counter-Reformation and into the largest Bible belt per capita in the world. This is one clue to the conundrum that has baffled so many people for over two decades.

The third and, depending upon your luck with the weather, possibly your most lasting impression will be of water; there is almost as much water in Ireland as there are green fields. Yet before you slump into depressing thoughts of rain-lashed windscreens, let me add that the real difficulty with Irish rain is its unpredictability. There are times of the year, however, particularly in May and June and again in September and early October when the weather can be as good as summer in Biarritz. The demonic feature of Irish rain is its sheer persistence; it can rain between 175 and 250 days in a year. Yet even then it has two saving graces; much rainfall is in the form of brief showers, often lit by startling rainbows; and much of the rest is feather-weight drizzle, what they call 'a soft day' in Ireland.

The miracle of all this water is that it has performed wonders for the Irish landscape, creating a shimmering network of lakes, many of them intricately dotted with Arcadian islands. One such is Yeats's Lough Gill with its Isle of Innisfree (there is a story that when a friend asked Yeats to show him the island, the poet could not remember which one it was). Ireland, in fact, has 920,000 acres of lakes and 9000 miles of rivers, which have given the country a delicate, haunting beauty all

its own. There are, I suppose, marvellous lakes all over the world – yet the sheer number and ubiquity of these quietly lapping waters, often the habitat of swan and a wide variety of wildfowl, is difficult to match else-where, and it gives Ireland an almost mystical patina of peace and tranquillity. The lakes and rivers make Ireland irresistible to anglers since they abound in fish, the coarse category including pike, perch, bream, rudd, tench, dace and hybrids. The finest locales are the Shannon and Erne rivers and tributaries, the River Barrow, the lakes of Monaghan and Meath, the River Blackwater, the Oranmore and Owenbeg rivers with their adjoining lakes in Sligo and the Moycullen lakes in Galway, which lie beside the vast expanse of Lough Corrib, Ireland's second largest lake. Game angling, too, is excellent sport with salmon, sea trout and brown trout relatively easy to catch; the waters of Connemara, Mayo and Donegal in particular are marvellous for sea trout. Loughs Corrib and Mask, incidentally among the most beautiful stretches of water in the country, are ideal for brown trout while, during the spring run, salmon weighing up to 20lbs can be taken along many coastal regions.

If anything, Irishmen could be accused of taking too great an interest in sport, although it is a mania stretching back into antiquity. Until the Norman Conquest the kings of Tara regularly staged a version of the Greek Olympics known as the Tailteann Games, which attracted athletes from all over the country. Irish sport can offer nothing so colourful or blood-thirsty as the Spanish bullfight but it does have Gaelic football and hurling; the latter, an ancient game played by Cuchulainn and other champions of the Heroic Age, is the world's fastest game played on turf. The country is littered with golf links; Dublin alone has nine but there are no fewer than 170 major courses or links throughout Ireland. Other activities formulated to use up leisure time have also been encouraged – cycling, motor-racing, hiking, bird-watching, paragliding and hang-gliding, orienteering, shooting, rock-climbing, windsurfing, canoeing, yachting, sub-aqua diving, surfing, water-skiing and, of course, anything to do with a horse. There are no fewer than thirty-six major hunts in Ireland, including such legendary combinations as the Meath and Kildare, the Galway Blazers and the Scarteen Black-and-Tans. In the 1870s the beautiful Empress Elizabeth of Austria, despite the disapproval of her cousin, Queen Victoria, preferred to hunt with the Meath rather than with the best in Leicestershire. The most glamorous and dashing horsewoman in Europe, she regularly brought twenty-one splendid hunters to Ireland, staying in great splendour at Summerhill, a magnificent Palladian mansion in Co. Meath owned by Lord Langford, and on her superb black horse, Domino, rode with a recklessness and daring that even the most hard-driving Irishman could not better. She aroused the kind of fascination among Irish country people that they reserve today for a pop idol, and they would travel miles just to glimpse her.

Horse-racing in its modern form was developed in Ireland by British Army cavalry officers and members of the Ascendancy. Today, Irish horse-racing and breeding compare well with the world's best. Dublin has two racecourses of its own and there are two more courses within easy reach: Fairyhouse, where the Irish Grand National is run every Easter Monday, and the great plain of The Curragh, in Kildare. The Irish Derby is reputed to be the richest horse-race in Europe and there is a constant Irish challenge to Longchamps and Auteuil for prestige if not for chic. There are twenty-eight other courses throughout Ireland with three hundred meetings held each year.

Ireland has always produced good natural food but until recently, with the bulk of the population enjoying the lowest standard of living outside the Eastern Bloc, there has been little opportunity to develop sophisticated cooking skills. And whether or not it was because their earliest ancestors had spent the first two thousand years of their sojourn catching and, presumably, eating fish, the Irish have always loathed it. Until Catholic observances were relaxed after Vatican II, most Irish turned to fish, and then only on Fridays, as a penance. Meanwhile, the Cork coast, for example, teemed with giant crabs and lobsters which were harvested by French fishermen who rushed them to the tables of Paris. Dublin Bay prawns and Galway oysters remained the preserve of the *cognoscenti*. Ireland's most famous native dishes were 'champ', mashed boiled potatoes whipped with milk, then covered with butter and spring onions (or scallions); Dublin Coddle, a none-too-appetizing mixture of streaky bacon and sausages; and the inevitable Irish stew, which was imported from Liverpool where it had been invented by poor Irish who had fled there after the Great Famine.

Dublin, though, which has always seen itself as a proper European metropolis (it was once, after all, the second city of the British Empire), has always been capable of producing eatable dishes provided you could pay for them. Even twenty years ago the country had awakened to the fact that it needed to exploit its natural resources and that food prepared according to the standards of Brussels or Rome had become mandatory. However, I do remember a critic writing of one fashionable restaurant: 'As the same diluted tomato ketchup appeared below the prawns in their cocktail, over the sirloin steak and unbelievably around a Chicken Maryland, none of the party had the courage to order a Pêche Melba'. Such a menu might have been a long way from the potatoes, soda bread and heavily salted bacon, accompanied by lashings of churned butter and boiled cabbage and washed down by tea as thick as Turkish coffee, that sustained most of the rural population, but it was scarcely enough for the gourmet. Today, however, levels in most Irish hotels and restaurants are exemplary, with many ingenious efforts being made to tempt jaded palates – although sea anemones might not be to everyone's taste.

Ireland, under the impetus of EEC membership and money, has undergone dramatic change in recent years. The old empty roads are no longer free of traffic; the picturesque donkey and cart appears to have gone; the red flannel petticoats and check shawls of the women in remote areas have been exchanged for tight trousers or jeans. Most disturbing of all to the eye of the traditionalist is the disappearance of the old cottage or cabin. Built of mortared stone, covered in whitewash and sometimes thatched, they offered a bedroom at each end and a cement-floored kitchen in the

middle; a turf fire was kept burning eternally in a great open hearth and heaps of dried turf were piled up against gabled walls outside. Now they are rapidly becoming a thing of the past and instead, blotting the landscape and still looking alien and savagely out of place, threatening to turn an ancient rural landscape into suburbia, are modern bungalows with lovingly tended gardens, TV aerials and all mod cons.

Yet Ireland still gives the appearance of being a happy, rousing sort of place. Everybody smiles at you; there is much laughter and jolliness; people are still kind and considerate and will happily spend an hour giving a lost motorist complex directions. Pious processions of men and women, old and young, still parade the streets of villages in the west at Corpus Christi, fervently reciting prayers, despite the stares of Japanese, German and American tourists, with a tinkling bell warning of the approach of the Blessed Sacrament held aloft by the parish priest in a great golden monstrance.

It is not easy, overall, and despite all the changes, to disagree with the summation of Donatus, the Irishman who became Bishop of Fiesole, near Florence, in the ninth century and who using the late Roman name for Ireland, wrote:

The noblest share of earth is the far western world
Whose name is written Scottia in the ancient books . . .

nor to resist the invitation expressed in a fourteenth-century Norman song which I believe still reflects the spirit of Ireland:

Ich am of Irlaunde
Am of the holy londe
Of Irlaunde;
Good sir, pray ye,
For of Saynte Charitee
Come and daunce wyt me
In Irlaunde

Traditional farming methods are still in use in remote areas. Here at Gweedore, Co. Donegal, a farmer tosses hay before building a cock.

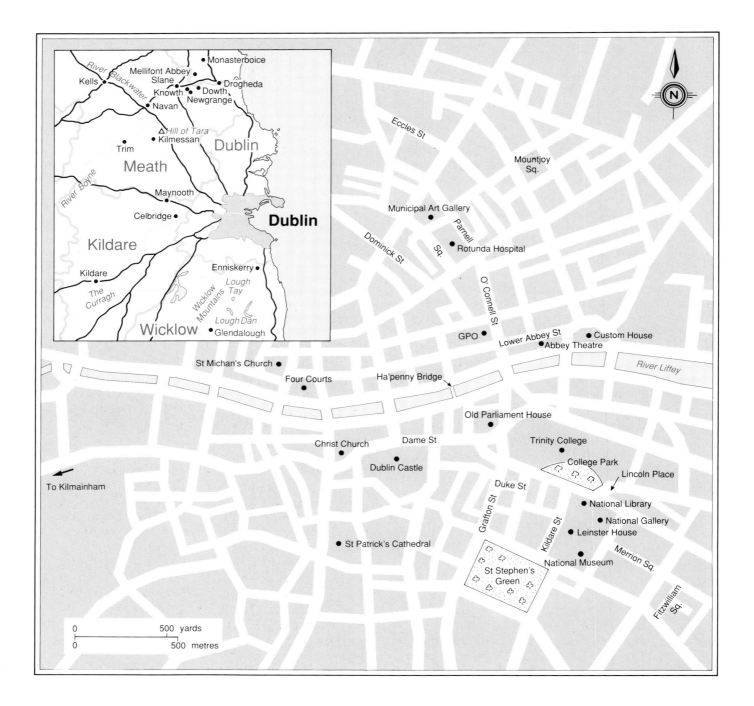

Inset map labels:

Monasterboice
Mellifont Abbey
Slane
Kells
River Blackwater
Knowth
Dowth
Drogheda
Newgrange
Navan
△ Hill of Tara
Kilmessan
Dublin
Trim
Meath
River Boyne
Maynooth
Celbridge
Dublin
Kildare
Kildare
The Curragh
Enniskerry
Lough Tay
Wicklow Mountains
Lough Dan
Wicklow
Glendalough

Main map labels:

Eccles St
Mountjoy Sq.
Municipal Art Gallery
Dominick St
Parnell Sq.
Rotunda Hospital
O'Connell St
GPO
Lower Abbey St
Custom House
Abbey Theatre
River Liffey
St Michan's Church
Four Courts
Ha'penny Bridge
Old Parliament House
Christ Church
Dame St
Trinity College
College Park
Lincoln Place
Dublin Castle
To Kilmainham
Duke St
National Library
Grafton St
National Gallery
Kildare St
Leinster House
Merrion Sq.
St Patrick's Cathedral
National Museum
St Stephen's Green
Fitzwilliam Sq.

0   500 yards
0   500 metres

N

1
Dublin and the Valley of the Kings

Dublin – Glendalough – Kildare – Drogheda
The Boyne Valley – Slane – Trim – Navan

The best way to approach Dublin is from the sea, the route chosen by the Norse Vikings who founded the city almost twelve hundred years ago. The city sits plumb in the middle of a sweeping, open-claw-like bay stretching almost twenty miles from the sentinel promontory of Howth Head in the north to Dalkey in the south. It appears at first as little more than a smudge low on the skyline but, behind it and running south, its dramatic backdrop slowly comes into view.

Few other capital cities are so gracefully overshadowed by heights. These are the delectable Wicklow Mountains, whose gentle slopes rise to a mixture of conical and boar-backed summits, the highest around 3000 feet. In the evening light of summer these great hills may be either a hazy blue or deep amethyst but nearly always, as cloud shadows jumble across them, they are dappled with golden green or even, where the dying light falls softly on the thick woods that tumble to the southern edge of the city, a luminous carmine. Drawing closer to Dublin, the omens, one decides, are good. Perhaps all the fables about this city are true; for is this not, among other things, Baghdad-on-the-Liffey, home of a thousand storytellers, the urban landscape of Molly Bloom, of Juno and the Paycock,

and of a motley collection of poets who have for centuries shed blood, including their own, dreaming of an impossible utopian beauty?

In AD 140 Ptolemy marked on his map of Ireland a site called Eblana, approximating to where Dublin now stands. By the eighth century some churches had taken root around a place on the River Liffey known in Irish as Baile Átha Cliath (baal-yeh-aha-klee) – that is, the Town of the Ford of Hurdles. That it was ever a town in any real sense is debatable – the Celts never built towns – and Dublin was born properly only in 841, when the Norsemen raised a defended place here which they called Dyfflin, a corruption of *dubh linn*, the Irish words meaning the Black or Dark Pool (presumably the Liffey, then as now, was a peat-like shade of brown not unlike stout). With the arrival of further forces under the splendidly named Ivar the Boneless in 852, the settlement was extended to the ridge above the river where Dublin Castle and Christ Church now stand, and the Vikings settled down to the real business of their lives which was trading and commerce; it is no coincidence that a Norse king of Dublin was the first to mint coins in Ireland. Dublin was the start of Irish urban life.

Strongbow, leader of the Norman invaders of Ireland, captured the town in 1171, settling its fate for the next 750 years. Ceded to the Crown the following year, it became the citadel of English power in the country, the heart of the Pale – that 'civilized' area subject to English law beyond which lurked the 'wild Irish'. In January 1922 English rule at last ended when Michael Collins, representing the first native government since the twelfth century, drove up to the walls of Dublin Castle, where once it had been usual to stick the heads of executed Irish 'traitors' on pikes, and where, once, the wife of a recalcitrant O'Neill chieftain was dangled in an iron cage until she starved; Collins then drove boldly through the main gate to accept the formal surrender of power from George V's Viceroy and give a very ancient nation a bright new beginning.

Today Dublin makes a fitful stab at being a proper capital with European pretensions, and neither completely succeeds nor utterly fails in the effort. When the famous Dublin Horse Show is in full spate at Ballsbridge or the European presidency falls to the Republic, one can have little doubt as to this city's international standing. The presence on the streets of Mercedes, Ferraris and Lamborghinis emphasizes this, as does the emergence of brittle young millionaires and entrepreneurs, many running intercontinental corporations. Still there, too, if rather more in the background these days, are the scions of old money, often to be seen hurrying up from their country estates to save more bits of old Dublin before developers raze it entirely. There is an enterprising clutch of five-star hotels and several superb restaurants as well as pubs reeking of atmosphere, where talk never ceases and people jig non-stop to the rhythms of live traditional music. You cannot deny that there is a lively, metropolitan scene.

And yet there remains an awkward tinge of provincialism to Dublin life – even if aspects of that life

The Ha'penny or Metal Bridge, Dublin, brings a Venetian whiff to the River Liffey, James Joyce's 'Anna Livia Plurabelle'.

make it one of the most civilized places on earth. Most of the city's problems, in fact, stem from a compound of relative poverty and philistinism; its burgeoning working class has, understandably, little but hours and wages on its mind and its continuing influx of 'culchies' – people straight from the farms – have little or no developed taste for urban living beyond pubs and discos. (The word 'culchie' is used disparagingly, particularly by Dubliners, to describe anyone from the country, or indeed anyone from outside Dublin.) Nor can Ireland engender the necessary wealth to sustain the city's traditions. As it is, the City Fathers, strapped for cash, are being constantly lambasted for furthering the destruction of a considerable architectural inheritance, and there are examples of criminal bad taste, and worse, all over the city. A chance to line pockets has also played its part, so it is not surprising that much of what was once a beautiful urban scene is vanishing fast. You will still find much to admire in Dublin, if also far too much that is likely to distress you. A saving measure, perhaps, is that you would have been even more distressed had you visited the city in the later stages of English domination. When the Irish Parliament was abolished in 1801 to make the United Kingdom of Great Britain and Ireland, most of the Ascendancy which had created the city's prosperity abandoned Dublin for London. At the same time, conditions in the Irish countryside having reached disaster proportions (the great Famine of the 1840s was succeeded by a brutal period of land clearance and evictions), hordes of starving people crowded in, adding to the crush of those who had already arrived in the eighteenth century. The resulting conditions were worse, if anything, than in Hogarth's London. The beautiful, if now deserted, Georgian squares and terraces on Dublin's north side sprouted dreadful tenements; it became an area of cracked windows and shattered fanlights, where stuccoed walls that had been built by Italian masters were left to the mercies of people eking out life in the depths of poverty and misery. So judgement on today's Dublin must be tempered, although nothing justifies much of the hard-nosed despoliation that has been permitted.

This city, however, has always been more than a collection of rose-bricked houses with superb Georgian doorways whose designs were originally conceived in Vicenza; it is also very much a state of mind. You can drive through the drabbest of suburbs (I exclude much of the south side of the Liffey, where there are still splendid Victorian and Edwardian mansions and long roads of well-proportioned Victorian terraces) and grow ever more depressed at the slovenliness, the cheap shops and amusement arcades, at examples of outright neglect comparable with the decay of St Petersburg, and yet you will rapidly find yourself drawn into the city's cosy, village-like embrace and lose your heart to it. For it is a city of great warmth and hospitality, with some of the most articulate and entertaining people in the world (even if there are those who hold that the sheer sharpness of tongue and malice inherent in the humour can be too much of a good thing). You will soon discover that it is a town where everybody seems to know everybody else, that there is much comic (or otherwise) story-telling, much intellectual vigour and endless opportunities for argument and debate, the more abstruse the better. Some years ago it was the practice of the literati (many truly eminent, many more merely *soi-disant*) to gather in a tavern which appears to have been a den of verbal piranhas along the lines of the Algonquin Round Table in New York; asked in his later years what subjects might have been discussed, the poet Patrick Kavanagh declared, 'Well, we'd debate how George Moore used the semi-colon in his novels.'

When you have ingested a tincture or two of comedy and more or less oriented yourself, eaten in a hostelry such as The Bailey in Duke Street, where at different times Parnell, Oliver St John Gogarty (the Buck Mulligan of Joyce's *Ulysses*) and even Joyce himself fêted themselves, and have crossed to Davy Byrne's pub (another Joycean relic), you may be in a better frame of mind to tolerate the visual eyesores and gaucheries that have disturbed your sense of good order.

Dublin reached its apogee in the eighteenth century when it was a thoroughly English town (I should add, however, that there existed a sharp distinction between the native-born Irish and those English who had settled in Ireland, best exemplified by the Duke of Wellington's declaration that he was not Irish — although his family had lived in the country for three centuries — but English, explaining, 'Just because a man is born in a stable, doesn't make him a horse'). A Commission for Making Wide and Convenient Streets saw the emergence of a city that, in V. S. Pritchett's words, 'might have been built out of the poetry of Pope': O'Connell Street was widened to 154 feet and extended to the river, two others were made 100 feet wide and another 96 feet wide. Beautiful buildings such as the Custom House, the Parliament House, the Four Courts, and additions to Trinity College which included one of the largest reading rooms in the world, rose alongside streets of elegant mansions. Lord Chesterfield, the Viceroy, laid out Phoenix Park (from the Irish *fionn uisce* meaning 'clear water') and opened it to the public; lying about a mile and a half upstream from O'Connell Bridge and extending some three miles along the Liffey, it covers 1800 acres and provides Dubliners with a city park that is among the largest anywhere, five times the size of London's Hyde Park.

The social whirl was equally impressive. For wit and pleasure, declared Lord Cloncurry, Dublin could be compared with Paris. In London, Horace Walpole confided to a friend, 'All the spirit or wit or poetry on which we subsist comes from Dublin'. With a population of two hundred thousand people, surpassed for size in the British Isles only by London, Dublin teemed with talented sculptors, artists, architects, wits, scientists, philosophers and eminent military men. There was an obverse side to the coin, of course; over three thousand taverns catered for the alcoholic addictions of the poor, who drank several millions of gallons of spirits every year, whiskey having come into universal

Georgian doorways, like this one in Merrion Square with its distinctive fanlight based on Italian models, still lend Dublin much of its grace and charm.

use. There were the wild 'bucks' of Dublin, sprigs of the Ascendancy, who indulged in orgies at a local Hellfire Club (based on Francis Dashwood's club in the caves at West Wycombe in southern England) and who turned performances at the theatres in Smock Alley and Crow Street into bear gardens, invading the stages so frequently that eventually soldiers with bayonets had to stand guard and spikes were erected along the footlights. Even these precautions failed to deter the wilder spirits, and the son of a duke castrated himself by attempting to jump on to the stage from his box.

Despite the city's rapid decline from real greatness, its conversational accomplishments were still in full spate towards the *fin-de-siècle* – 'the rich Dublin talk that astonished London when it was first heard on the lips of Wilde'. The town had become a place, according to Gogarty, where 'every man is a potential liar, poet or friend'. The Countess of Fingall recalled, 'I cannot count the number of wits and storytellers of those days; you saw men buttonholing each other everywhere just to tell stories and then roaring with laughter'. The streets swirled with men of genius.

John Pentland Mahaffy, Provost of Trinity College at the turn of the century, is said to have been the greatest conversationalist Dublin ever produced (his bon mots, alas, have been devalued by time and imitation). Sir Shane Leslie, Winston Churchill's cousin, once said, 'Until you heard Mahaffy talk you hadn't realized how language could be used to charm and hypnotize. With this gift there were no doors which could not be opened, no society which was proof against its astonishing effect. Kings and queens, famous men and beautiful women, all must come under its powerful and compelling spell.' The splendour of Mahaffy's wit was such that he became a regular guest of the Kaiser. Wilde called him, 'A really great talker, an artist in vivid words'. When a suffragette once

The seventeenth-century Royal Hospital, Kilmainham, is the largest building of its period in Ireland. It now houses the Irish Museum of Modern Art.

bearded Mahaffy, fiercely demanding to know, 'Well, what *is* the difference between a man and a woman?', Mahaffy countered instantly, 'I can't conceive'.

Pritchett describes the Dublin talker as 'an exhausting professional of whom a little is a pleasure', and J. P. Donleavy, author of *The Ginger Man*, hits the nail on the head precisely when he says that 'Dubliners get on stage and take starring roles . . . they turn conversation into a combination of insult and rumour . . .', and that Dublin is said to be 'famous for producing writers but it's simply that the writers are failed talkers . . . who, emotionally bruised, sneak away from the ridicule to write and get their revenge'.

Physically, modern Dublin is a considerable sprawl and most of its suburbs are unremittingly drear, although to the north of the city, Howth with the 560-foot Ben of Howth and Malahide with the magnificent Talbot castle, and to the south Dun Laoghaire, Dalkey and Killiney, are all worth a saunter. Historic Dublin covers a small area, most of it walkable. The density of historic associations and important buildings is such, however, that I can only hope to steer you towards a small personal selection.

It is worth making the journey of a mile and a bit along the south bank of the River Liffey to Kilmainham, where you will see Ireland's oldest surviving fully classical building and the largest seventeenth-century structure in the country. This is the superb Royal Hospital, which was founded by the Duke of Ormonde under a 1680 charter from Charles II to provide a hospice for pensioner soldiers. A magnificent, only slightly scaled-down, version of Les Invalides, it adds much to the adornment of Dublin. It has now been put to excellent use, housing the Irish Museum of Modern Art, something that Irish art lovers had been striving for since the early 1900s, when the art dealer Sir Hugh Lane first whetted their appetites with an exhibition of Impressionist and Abstract art. Most familiar names are on display but what adds real bite to the collection is work by such outstanding Irish artists as Jack B. Yeats, Louis le Brocquy and others. You can also, in a sense, kill two birds by visiting the old Kilmainham Gaol where Parnell was once incarcerated in an effort to halt violence in the Irish countryside; derelict for years, the gaol has been refurbished by volunteer efforts and is now emerging as a national shrine. It was here that the leaders of the 1916 Rebellion were executed, and the courtyard where they were shot, the badly wounded James Connolly strapped to a chair so that he could be targetted, still exudes a hauntingly eerie feeling. You can also see the small chapel where at 1.30 a.m. on 4 May 1916, Miss Grace Gifford stood waiting until the already dying Joseph Plunkett was brought in hand-cuffed, and then by the light of a single candle and with twenty British soldiers lining the walls with fixed bayonets, married him, only to be hurried away immediately the ceremony was over. Just before dawn she was permitted to see him in his cell, again with a party of British soldiers present, before he was led away to his execution.

On your way back to the city centre you might like to cross the river and visit St Michan's, one of Dublin's oldest churches (although most of the present fabric dates from the seventeenth century), where you can indulge in the slightly grisly ritual of shaking hands with the extraordinarily well-preserved remains of three long-dead people, one of whom is alleged to have been a Crusader. Kept deep in the church vaults, the bodies appear to have been preserved in the bog air. Shaking hands is supposed to bring you good luck.

O'Connell Street was, until recently, the city's showpiece but has now become tawdry and is even dangerous after dark. While none of Dublin was conceived on quite the Napoleonic scale of Haussman's Paris, the spaciousness and grandeur of O'Connell Street was something that London, for instance, might have envied. Its decline dates from 1916, when it was shelled during the Easter Rebellion that eventually led to Irish independence; then in 1922 further portions were wrecked during the Civil War between the newly established Free State and Republican 'Irregulars' who refused to accept the Treaty with Britain. In 1966, the then moribund IRA sprang to life and incompetently half-blew up the great 134-foot Doric pillar to Nelson, raised thirty-two years before the old sea-dog's column in Trafalgar Square and the Irish Army had to complete the job, depriving Dublin of a notable focal point.

The finest building in the street is the GPO, *the* shrine of Irish nationalism. A classical structure with an Ionic portico, it was designed by the notable Francis Johnston and erected between 1815 and 1817. It owes its sanctified position to the fact that it was the GHQ of Patrick Pearse and James Connolly during the Rising. Only when the building had been set on fire did the 'rebels' decide to abandon it. Although the interior was gutted, the façade and portico in front of which Pearse had read out the Declaration of an Irish Republic were saved, and the building reopened for business in 1929. In 1934 an impressive statue, the *Death of Cuchulainn* by Oliver Sheppard, was erected in the main hall to honour the dead and emphasize the link between Pearse and Ireland's heroic Celtic past.

The Rotunda, just up the street, is now a maternity hospital, but was once a concert hall and ballroom where in the past there were performances by Michael Kelly, Mozart's friend (and the first Don Basilio in *Figaro*), John Field, Glinka's tutor and the inventor of the nocturne, and Franz Liszt himself; once, after a concert here, Paganini scattered gold coins among the starving throng who had gathered to see him. You can wander through the heart of O'Casey land near Mountjoy Square, see Belvedere House (now a Jesuit school), the setting for the sermon on Hell in Joyce's *A Portrait of the Artist as a Young Man*, and stroll past St George's church where Wellington married Kitty Pakenham and lived unhappily ever after, the bride's face having been blemished by smallpox; you can see Eccles Street, where Molly Bloom fantasized her famous soliloquy in *Ulysses*, or the house in Dominick Street where Sir William Rowan Hamilton, discoverer of quaternions, whose work led to the quantum theory and advances in nuclear physics, was born. But one could linger in street after street in Dublin and here it is possible only to look at the bare essentials. The Municipal Art Gallery in Parnell Square deserves your attention. The building itself, Charlemont House, was erected in the 1760s for James Caulfield, Earl of

Charlemont, who had done much to achieve self-government for the old Irish Parliament. A highly cultivated figure of much talent and liberal sympathies, Caulfield was a patron of the arts on a grand scale, having travelled widely through Europe, and his house soon became known as 'The Holland House of Dublin'. Charlemont House now displays thirty pictures from the Sir Hugh Lane collection. Sir Hugh, nephew of that Lady Gregory who was the principal source of the Irish literary revival of the turn of the century, was drowned in the Lusitania in 1915; because a codicil to his will was never witnessed, a bitter legal wrangle between Dublin and London ensued over ownership of the collection, which includes work by Manet, Courbet and Monet. The matter has been temporarily resolved but a new agreement will have to be reached in 1993.

There is a new Abbey Theatre nowadays in Lower Abbey Street, replacing the famous old house on the site of the Dublin morgue which had burned out in 1951. The old theatre was the scene of great uproar in its time, largely reflecting the clash between Holy Ireland and the new secularism. When *The Countess Cathleen* was first performed there in 1899, the author, W. B. Yeats, was accused of 'revolting blasphemies'. And the first performance of Synge's great play *The Playboy of the Western World* actually provoked a riot both inside and outside the theatre. When O'Casey's *The Plough and the Stars* opened in 1926 there was more mayhem; shouting, booing, whistling and singing were followed by the throwing of chairs, shoes, tomatoes, apples, eggs and stink bombs, and culminated in a mob invading the stage and fighting with the actors. When the police finally restored order Yeats strode from the wings and castigated the audience in astonishingly high-flown terms: 'You have disgraced yourselves again! Is this to be the ever-recurring celebration of the arrival of Irish genius? Synge first and now O'Casey . . . Dublin has once more rocked the cradle of genius. From such a scene in this theatre went forth the fame of Synge. Equally the fame of O'Casey is born here tonight. This is his apotheosis!' O'Casey himself later admitted he had no idea what 'apotheosis'

meant 'until I looked it up in the dictionary – but it sounded grand!'

The Custom House, which is only a short distance away, is not only one of Dublin's two finest buildings (the other is the Four Courts) but is among the finest in Europe, and helps to give Dublin the architectural edge over such rivals as Edinburgh. Its architect was James Gandon, a Londoner of Huguenot and Welsh extraction who was invited to Dublin by the Earl of Charlemont. The original idea was to match London's Somerset House but in the event Gandon surpassed it. He chose a Palladian style with baroque elements and used granite and Portland stone. (The latter had to be replaced by Ardbraccan stone from Co. Meath during reconstruction work after the IRA set fire to the building in 1921 to destroy British records and render British administration impossible; the fire raged for five days and left the noble building a mere shell). Ironically there had been much controversy over its original construction because John Beresford, Chief of the Irish Revenue, who commissioned the building, was much hated and Gandon himself had to use his sword to protect himself during the work. There was undisguised glee when it was realized that Beresford had chosen a muddy site on the Liffey and it was forecast that the building would sink; however Gandon laid his foundations on a layer of pine planks and the scheme worked. When finished in 1791, it was hailed as the greatest building in the British Isles by any architect since Wren. The south front has a fine Doric portico with outstanding sculptures and masks; the north front has a smaller portico with statues of the Continents. The beautifully proportioned central copper dome rises 125 feet and is topped by a statue of Commerce by Edward Smyth, Gandon's favourite sculptor. Cleaned in 1991, it has to be viewed from the opposite side of the Liffey; personally I find it breathtaking.

A delightful saunter (if you can stand the car fumes) along the river, past O'Connell Bridge and the Metal Bridge – or Ha'penny Bridge because there was once a toll there – a delicate structure that might have strayed from Venice, will give you a chance to savour Dublin's

special quality. Old commercial buildings are reflected in the Liffey, and church towers and variously shaped temples of commerce fade softly into the distance, altogether a light and airy prospect. Like Gandon's first Dublin masterpiece, the Four Courts can be properly appreciated only from the south side of the river. Its vast and distinctive lantern dome is an unforgettable sight. Work began in 1786, and it took Gandon sixteen years to erect the central block, with its portico of six Corinthian columns, and the radiating courts of the Exchequer, Common Pleas, King's Bench and Chancery, complete with two quadrangles and various wings. In 1922 Irregulars seized the building but Michael Collins, using artillery borrowed from the British, decided to bombard them and forced them to evacuate. The Irregulars planted mines which exploded after they left and created considerable damage, in particular destroying Ireland's Public Record Office and its contents, still a sore loss.

I suggest you now climb the incline, which was part of the original Norse settlement, to the ridge above. You might look in at The Brazen Head, said to be Dublin's oldest pub and known to have been the haunt of Robert Emmet (1778–1803), one of the most romantic of Irish patriots, and of the United Irishmen, a group of whom were seized there during the 1798 rebellion. An alternative route is by Fishamble Street, famed as the site of the Concert hall where on 13 April 1742 Handel's *Messiah* was given its first performance. Annoyed by London's preference for a rival composer, Handel accepted an invitation from the Duke of Devonshire, then Viceroy of Ireland, to compose a new work for Dublin. Handel took six weeks to write the great Oratorio, which was first heard in the old Charitable Musical Society's Hall, now long since vanished. Altogether he spent a year in Dublin, meeting the by-then demented Swift, and made London

The Custom House, James Gandon's first Irish commission. Intended to rival Somerset House, London, it is considered Dublin's most beautiful building.

wait two years before it could hear his great work, a savage revenge.

Christ Church warrants a visit because it is Dublin's oldest building, although little of the original structure remains. It was founded in 1040 but added to by Strongbow and St Laurence O'Toole (whose machinations did much to promote Henry II's claim, under a papal bull, to be Lord of Ireland). Here the pretender Lambert Simnel was crowned Edward VI in 1487. The great tower which is a feature of the modern building dates only from 1600. The cathedral's clergy turned Anglican in 1551 but mass was again celebrated within its walls during the reign of James II. By 1829, however, the place had become so dilapidated that it had to close its doors. Wholesale restoration, including the erection of the present east wing and work on the west front, flying buttresses, baptistry and Synod Hall, with its covered connecting bridge, was carried out thanks to the philanthrophy of a Dublin distiller, and the much-changed cathedral re-opened in 1878. Strongbow is said to be buried near the south nave where there is an alleged effigy of him. In a side chapel St Laurence O'Toole's embalmed heart is preserved in a bronze, heart-shaped case suspended on a chain. Perhaps the most impressive sight of all is the ancient vaulted crypt, among the largest in the British Isles, where markets were held in medieval times and taverns were open for business as late as the seventeenth century.

St Patrick's Cathedral, although it dates from 1191 and, at 300 feet long, is Ireland's largest church, cannot be compared with any of the marvels of English cathedral architecture. The building sits on the site of a pre-Norman church said to have been where Patrick himself baptized converts, and has undergone much restoration due to the generosity of the Guinness family. Having been used by Cromwell as a stables and by James II as a barracks, after many vicissitudes it has now become the Church of Ireland's (Protestant) national cathedral. Its interior is impressive and the Jacobean memorial to the first Earl of Cork (father of Boyle the physicist) is the largest in the British Isles. These is also a memorial to Turlough O'Carolan, the

famed eighteenth-century harpist and composer of Gaelic music, and a tablet commemorating the Revd Charles Wolfe who wrote *The Burial of Sir John Moore*.

The cathedral's main source of interest, of course, is its associations with Jonathan Swift, whose grave lies in the south aisle alongside that of 'Stella' (his friend Esther Johnson who lived with him for many years and is believed to have married him secretly). She stayed with him despite his affair with Esther Vanhomrigh ('Vanessa') which ended only with the latter's death. Above the entrance to the nearby robing room is his famous epitaph, which is a reflection of his love for the Irish poor, his indignation at the injustices heaped on them and his championship of the Irish nation against England (he once advised the Irish: 'Burn everything English except their coal!'). When flooding of the cathedral exposed certain coffins in 1835, Swift's and 'Stella's' were opened and the skulls examined by Sir William Wilde, father of Oscar, who diagnosed the source of Swift's pain and dementia as Ménière's syndrome. Among others buried here are Schomberg, who fell leading William III's forces at the Battle of the Boyne.

Dublin Castle once bore the same grim reputation in Ireland as the Tower of London in England. Almost nothing of the thirteenth-century original remains and what stands today is, essentially, yet another product of the prolific eighteenth century. By that time the castle had ceased to be a scene of torture, death or imprisonment (one of the great romances of Irish history is the daring escape from the Bermingham Tower of the great Gaelic chieftain Red Hugh O'Donnell, who had been tricked into captivity by the Lord Deputy). Instead, it became the hub of fashionable society, and much effort was spent by the great hostesses of the day (including the famous Theresa, Lady Londonderry) in obtaining invitations to the

The Four Courts, second of Gandon's masterpieces. Its distinctive lantern dome was bombarded when held by 'Irregulars' during the 1920s Civil War.

various balls, presentations, dinners and soirées held there by the Viceroys. Victoria and Albert danced quadrilles here during their 1849 visit to Ireland and George V resided in the castle during his visit in 1911.

The state apartments are, indeed, quite sumptuous. The most magnificent is St Patrick's Hall, a glorious setting for presidential inaugurations and state receptions. The ceiling decorations may appear a trifle ironical today, depicting as they do the benefits England had allegedly showered on Ireland – an idea the Irish, rightly or wrongly, have since vehemently repudiated. The Record Tower in Lower Court is the only surviving Norman structure, one of the original four towers. The early nineteenth-century Chapel Royal by Francis Johnston is an architectural gem. Once dedicated to the Irish version of Anglicanism, it is now a Catholic church (Handel is said to have played on its organ). The Bedford Tower, in Upper Yard, houses the Heraldic Museum and for a fee will help trace any Irish ancestors you may have. It is also the site of a great unsolved mystery worthy of Sherlock Holmes. Just prior to the visit of Edward VII in 1907, the Irish Crown Jewels (a set of jewelled regalia) were stolen from the safe here; despite intensive inquiries they have never been recovered nor the culprit found.

A gentle stroll will now take you down Dame Street, once the main axis of the city, and towards two more magnificent buildings. Ahead of you rises the great 300-foot-long Palladian façade of Trinity College, fronted by statues of Burke and Goldsmith, and on your left, at the corner of College Green, is the old Irish Parliament House (now the Bank of Ireland). Here, in May 1782, Henry Grattan, leader of the 'Irish Protestant nation', following his triumph in forcing Britain to repeal ancient laws whereby Ireland was bound by Westminster, ringingly declared, 'Ireland is now a nation!' Eighteen years later, amid riots, acts of gross corruption and venality, his words were made a mockery when the Irish Parliament voted its own abolition and Ireland became part of the new United Kingdom. Admission to some of the rooms of the old Parliament House is possible, accompanied by liveried attendants. On view are a spectacular eighteenth-

century chandelier and two gigantic tapestries depicting the Siege of Derry and the Battle of the Boyne; the old Irish House of Lords can also be seen, as well as a magnificent ceiling by the Italian Francini brothers who did much of Dublin's fine stucco work; their Venus here was the first full-scale human figure achieved in Irish stucco.

Trinity College is an Elizabethan foundation dating from 1591 and built on the site of an Augustinian priory. Socially, at least, it stands immediately behind Oxbridge in the pecking order of universities in the British Isles. Founded with the idea of weaning the Irish from Catholicism, it was not freed from religious restrictions until 1873 and until relatively recently was still shunned by Irish Catholics. Today, however, over seventy per cent of students are Catholic. For all its undoubted charms and fine buildings, many in classical style – it has been likened to a Cambridge college – it is too grey and austere for my taste to rival Oxbridge, although the campanile, which was erected by Sir Charles Lanyon in the main quadrangle in 1853, is a spectacular sight as you walk through the main gateway. Sitting as it does in twenty-five acres in the very heart of Dublin, Trinity is, nevertheless, a beautiful and restful place and, with a roll-call of students that includes some of the greatest names in Irish (even British) history, it radiates an intense aura.

The real treasures of Trinity, however, are housed in the college's magnificent 209-foot-long library which is lit by a hundred windows. This superb room holds five thousand manuscripts and more than two million printed books. Here, among other priceless texts, are displayed two jewels that would attract visitors to Ireland even if there were nothing else to see. The first is the Book of Durrow, a seventh-century illuminated gospel book in Irish majuscule script, from the Columban monastery of Durrow, Co. Offaly. The jewel

The Chapel Royal, Dublin Castle, where English monarchs once prayed. The organ, according to tradition, was played upon by Handel.

Christ Church Cathedral, heavily restored, stands on the hill used by the Viking Ostmen to build the first settlement at Dublin. It is Dublin's oldest building.

of jewels, of course, is the Book of Kells, a late eighth-century gospel which was begun in Columcille's own monastery on Iona but was probably completed in another Columban foundation at Kells, Co. Meath, where it was preserved until the seventeenth century. As Iona was a wholly Irish foundation, and remained so throughout its existence, although both Saxon and British monks became part of its community, the Book cannot be seen as anything other than a product of Irish tradition, whether or not any, all or only part of it was painted in Ireland. The script itself is written in the beautiful round uncial of all the best Irish manuscripts. The whole thing possesses a magnificent flamboyance and an exuberant quality that is expressed in a continuous change of ornamentation running through the text. The capitals at the start of each

paragraph are emblazoned with brightly coloured entwinements of birds, snakes, distorted and attenuated men and quadrupeds, fighting or performing all sorts of acrobatic feats. Animals wander crazily about the pages between the lines or on top of them. It is both wholly profound and highly amusing and represents the apex of Celtic art. The book is made up of a total of 680 pages, but in 1953 it was divided into four volumes and re-bound (the original, highly decorated cover was lost centuries ago when the book was stolen). Two volumes are always on show, one opened at a full-page illumination, the other showing a page full of the exuberant little figures. Each day another page is turned.

A walk across College Park will bring you out on Lincoln Place, where you will find yourself ravished by the choices ahead. If painting interests you, the National Gallery has an excellent collection; you will find work by Fra Angelico, Titian, Tintoretto, Bellini, Correggio and Canaletto as well as by El Greco, Goya, Rubens, Brueghel, Rembrandt and many others; as you are in Ireland you may, however, be more interested in the work of indigenous painters such as Nathaniel Hone, James Barry, J. B. Yeats (W. B.'s brother), Sir William Orpen and Walter Osborne. The gallery is part of a complex embracing Leinster House (the Irish Parliament), the Natural History Museum, the National College of Art, the National Library and the National Museum. Leinster House, which faces west to Kildare Street, was built in 1746 for the Earl of Kildare, later the Duke of Leinster. In 1815 it was sold to the Royal Dublin Society, which was moved to Ballsbridge in 1922 to make way for Parliament (Dáil Éireann). Designed by Richard Castle (a German originally called Cassels) in a rather glum Ardbraccan stone, Leinster House is often claimed by Dubliners to have been the prototype of Washington's White House, which was

An ornate lamp-post in College Green, Dublin. Behind is the curving façade of the Bank of Ireland, once the Irish Parliament House until union with Britain in 1800.

This striking 100-foot campanile in Trinity College dates only from 1853. The college was founded by Elizabeth I in the hope of 'civilizing' the Catholic Irish.

built by the Irishman James Hoban. Their claim appears to be based solely on the knowledge that Hoban trained in Dublin, for the resemblance is slight.

The Irish, despite the sorrow that threads so much of their history, are really as proud as Spaniards and rather resent the image that their homeless, starving masses took with them to Britain and the United States in the nineteenth century. The glorious contents of the National Museum do something to explain the origins of this stubborn pride. Here is a repository of ancient treasure unique and certainly worthy of its fame. Many of the early artefacts, dating back to the Stone and Bronze Ages, may be pre-Celtic but they are still Irish, still part of the national consciousness. The truly marvellous gold torques, lunulae, fibulae and miniature chariots and boats may have been fashioned two

thousand years before Christ by craftsmen who came to Ireland from the Mediterranean, but these settlers were assimilated into the races that constitute the Irish people and their genes linger on. The gold itself was dug out of Irish earth. Among the outstanding relics is the Feakle Treasure, dating from 650 BC, which was unearthed as recently as 1943.

But it is from early Christian art that possibly the greatest treasures derive, dating from that brief but ennobling period when Irish art, culture and scholarship were triumphant in north-western Europe, constituting the finest artistic flowering outside Byzantium and Moorish Spain. Here then are the eighth-century Ardagh Chalice, the penannular Tara Brooch, the Moylough belt-shrine made of silvered bronze with enamel appliqué, the beautifully decorated bronze Shrine of St Patrick's Bell and the great processional Cross of Cong, commissioned by the last high king of Ireland for Cong Abbey in Mayo, as well as other precious relics. Worth seeing, too, is the collection of Irish silver, glass and furniture, which are quite distinctive.

Perhaps the time has now arrived to simply stroll around the city and drink in what is left of its old glories. Merrion Square, for all its decay and neglect, is Georgian Dublin at its most theatrical; the doorways, in particular, though some are shamefully neglected, are still beautiful. Oscar Wilde was born at no. 1; Daniel O'Connell owned no. 58; Yeats lived for a while at no. 52. At no. 24 Upper Merrion Street the Duke of Wellington was born. Oddly, there are few churches in the area, but at the end of Upper Mount Street stands the striking pepper-pot church of St Stephen's. A short distance south is Fitzwilliam Square, now the Harley Street of Dublin and another Georgian showpiece.

Your walk is almost over as you turn back into St Stephen's Green, first and largest of the city's great squares. At the centre is a magnificent park laid out in 1880 by Sir Arthur Guinness (later Lord Ardilaun) and gifted to the city, serving the needs of central Dublin in much the same way as Hyde Park serves London, or Central Park New York, although it is tiny by comparison. It remains impressive despite the non-stop whirr of traffic around its wide-avenued perimeter and the destruction of many fine houses by developers. The old Guinness town house, no. 80, was once the centre of fashionable Dublin society, while at nos. 85 and 86, now called Newman House and part of University College, Gerard Manley Hopkins taught and Newman himself was Rector when the institution was later founded in 1909 as the first university for Catholics in Ireland. Newman House is open to visitors and has fine interiors. You may now like to stroll through the park to the Shelbourne Hotel, Ireland's most celebrated hostelry, haunt of the old Ascendancy and now patronized by well-known guests from all over the world, and either enjoy an excellent meal or merely sip an Irish coffee while you gaze out at the park; the scene of intense action during the Easter Rebellion, it was here that Constance Markievicz (one of Yeats's famous 'two girls in silk kimonos'), who became the first women in Europe to be elected to Parliament, shot a man dead. When you leave the Shelbourne, walk down Grafton Street ('Dublin's Bond Street'), admire the shop windows (which are not really on a par with Bond Street's) and ease your tired feet in Bewley's, a great Dublin institution where you can linger over coffee and cakes or, indeed, other fancies, and imagine yourself, perhaps, in Vienna.

The countryside to the south of the city is all within such easy reach of St Stephen's Green that, in a sense, you are quite unprepared for its sudden wildness and remoteness. It is as though you had stepped through glass into another time and place, into a landscape of golden gorse and purple heather, dark bogs and long waves of sighing grass, and bosky valleys with frisky lambs and sheep enclosed by gently contoured hills. Granite outcrops, left exposed when the Ice Age scraped away the detritus of slate and schists that had been deposited there from the original Caledonian

Rising in places to over 3000 ft, the Wicklow Mountains with their rugged moors, deep-green glens and glorious lakes lie within easy reach of Dublin.

folding, lie on either side of the long, windswept road to evocative Glendalough, deep in the Wicklow Mountains with, at many times of the year, not a soul in sight. It is almost like leaving Piccadilly Circus and within fifteen minutes finding yourself in the Highlands of Scotland.

On the way to Glendalough you pass though Enniskerry, a pretty enough village which owes its limited charms largely to planning by the Powerscourt estate on whose demesne it stands. Just beyond the village, and set amid fourteen thousand fertile acres, stand the ruins of Powerscourt House, which until 1974 was among the loveliest of Ireland's eighteenth-century country mansions. Built on the site of an ancient castle of the O'Tooles (who along with the O'Byrnes were part of that nation of 'wild Irish' who constantly swooped on Dublin or otherwise harried The Pale) the house, on the eve of being opened to the public after much restoration, was gutted by fire in 1974. For a country which, during the revolution and civil war, lost so much of whatever excellent architecture it possessed, this was catastrophe.

Fortunately what remains is still worth seeing: set amid breathtakingly beautiful scenery overlooked by the Great and Little Sugar Loaf mountains, the formal gardens are superb. A well-laid-out perron descends from a terrace floored by pebbles and ornamented by statues towards a natural lake, which has been sympathetically transformed into a Triton Pool. Further on is a splendid arboretum with monkey puzzles, eucalyptus and sitka spruce. Lying some distance from these delights is a deer park and – the *pièce de résistance* – the Powerscourt Waterfall, at 400 feet the highest in the British Isles. the water tumbles down through a narrow glade with a roar that almost stuns you.

The road south then takes you up through the Sally Gap to Roundwood, Laragh and finally Glendalough; your eye is caught by the summits of War Hill, Djouce Mountain, Mullaghcleevaun and Tonduff, all around 2000 feet, and, some distance ahead, Lugnaquilla, which at over 3000 feet is Ireland's third highest mountain. On the way you pass two small romantic-looking corries, Lough Dan and Lough Tay (or Luggala), both of which can be glimpsed from the road. Luggala is owned by Garech de Brun of the Guinness family (a noted Dublin host and patron of the arts) whose estate is roamed by a herd of Sitka deer. Just before Laragh you descend into the Annamoe Valley where, at the age of seven, Laurence Sterne had a lucky escape from death when he fell into a mill-race.

It is easy enough to complain that Glendalough, a mere thirty-two miles from Daniel O'Connell's statue overlooking O'Connell Bridge, has been ruined – and it is true that in comparison with what it was like when I first visited it before World War II, much of its magic has been dissipated, mainly because of the press of trippers and tourists that now crowd into this beautiful valley: once upon a time the entire essence of the place was a blissful calm and an unbroken solitude, and Glendalough, like most of the world's great beauty spots, has not escaped the destructive trample of feet.

The name itself means The Glen of the Two Lakes – but it is the upper one that is by far the most magical. Ringed by the steeply wooded slopes of mountains just over 2000 feet high, this small lake remains, in my view, an enchanted stretch of water. It was here in 545, before the foundation of such famed monastic settlements as Clonmacnoise and Bangor, that St Kevin, scion of the royal house of Leinster, founded a small hermitage now called Tempull-na-Skellig (Church of the Rock); it stands on the south side of the lake, on an artificially levelled platform in a cliff, and can be reached only by boat. Higher up this cliff, and almost inaccessible, is St Kevin's Bed, where the hermit is alleged to have slept. Local legend has it that, pursued by a young woman, he tried to find a place where she could not reach him but awoke one morning to find her beside him. In true Celtic saintly fashion, he at once pushed her into the lake.

Kevin has been called the Irish Francis of Assisi, for

Glendalough – the Valley of the Two Lakes – is one of Ireland's best-loved landscapes. The monastery here was founded by St Kevin in 545.

he had an extraordinary rapport with wild creatures. It is said that he was supplied daily with fresh salmon brought to him by an otter as he stood waist-deep in icy water reading his breviary. On one occasion a blackbird alighted on his outstretched hand and began building her nest; Kevin, as a penance, allowed the nest to remain there until the eggs had hatched.

Much of what is wonderful about Glendalough is encompassed by this lovely, shimmering lake and I advise you to seek out a quiet place, sit down and simply allow its ancient balm to flow over you.

There is much more to the place, of course, than its serenity. Kevin's disciples built his foundation into one of the great seats of learning of early medieval Europe; the monastic settlement is further down the valley, towards its entrance, and immediately before one reaches the first, smaller lake. Entering Glendalough, the first thing you see is a hotel which once enjoyed the patronage of Edward VII, and just beside it a ruined gateway comprising two arches, the only surviving example of an early Irish monastic gateway, leading to the monastic *civitates* or 'city'. Through it you will find a ninth-century cathedral, a twelfth-century St Kevin's Cross (unfinished) and a thirteenth-century priest's house, above the door of which is carved a figure that appears to be a representation of Kevin himself. Further down the slope is what most people have come to see – the two-storeyed oratory called St Kevin's Kitchen, approximately 23 feet by 15 feet, with a steeply inclined roof and a small bell-turret or round tower. Against a backdrop of wooded hills and glittering water, it is a memorable sight with much of architectural interest. To the north-west rises a magnificent 110-foot round tower where monks once took refuge when Vikings devastated the valley. In 1398 this lovely, innocent place, with its Celtic crosses, incised slab-stones and often intricate

The restored Long Gallery at Castletown House, Co. Kildare, its walls a riot of Pompeian colours. The great chandeliers are of Murano glass.

The Print Room, Castletown House, dates from 1768, and is one of the earliest examples of a fashion for applying favourite prints directly to the walls.

romanesque decoration, was again ravaged when the English of Dublin attacked it. Finally, when the sixteenth-century Tudor reconquest of Ireland destroyed what was left of the old Gaelic order, Glendalough was also laid in ruins. It was not until the beginning of the nineteenth century that the remains were excavated to make the valley one of Ireland's most cherished places.

Returning to Dublin and this time leaving the city by the main road to the west, you will come first to Maynooth, which is little more than an outer suburb of the capital. Much of the interest here centres on St Patrick's College, the greatest Catholic seminary in these islands, which has supplied priests and bishops to all parts of the world. St Patrick's was founded in 1795 by the English authorities at the instigation of

Edmund Burke, who argued that the anti-Catholic laws and restrictions then in force meant that young Irishmen were being forced to seek an education in France and were therefore imbibing French revolutionary ideas. The considerable complex consists primarily of two huge squares, one Palladian, the other Gothic, to a design by Pugin. The chapel is a fine Gothic Revival work by J. J. McCarthy, a leading designer of the day, and has the tallest spire in the country. The rest of the architecture is nondescript but the museum is worth a visit, although the bulk of the exhibits are of an ecclesiastical character. However, there is an Ecce Homo rescued from Cromwell's sack of Drogheda and some church vestments made by Marie-Antoinette's ladies-in-waiting. Another superb set of vestments decorated with shamrocks was the gift of Empress Elizabeth of Austria (whose portrait hangs in the dining hall — a startling sight among so many celibates). The empress first sent the college a magnificent silver statue of St George, but when it was tactfully pointed out that she had got the wrong saint for this place, she donated the vestments instead.

At the opposite end of Maynooth's main street lies Carton, the former home of the dukes of Leinster, where Victoria and Albert stayed during their 1849 visit to Ireland; because of many changes of ownership it is not always open to the public. The house was remodelled by Richard Castle who died during the course of the work and was buried in the manorial church which stands just within the gates of St Patrick's, near the massive ruins of a great castle of the earls of Kildare, parts of which date to 1203. Later, the architect Richard Morrison somewhat spoiled Castle's work by reversing the front and back of the house and adding a Regency dining room, but the state apartments are superb, with ceilings decorated by the ubiquitous Francini brothers.

Almost at hand to the south-east of Maynooth is Celbridge, part of a small network of places worth seeing within a thirteen-mile drive of Dublin. Celbridge Abbey is significant because of its associations with Swift; it was once owned by a Dutchman called Vanhomrigh who arrived in Ireland as Commissary

General with William III's army and was the father of Swift's 'Vanessa'. A seat down by the river is the idyllic spot where the couple lingered during his frequent visits to the abbey. In the end they parted and she left her considerable fortune not to Swift but to Bishop Berkeley.

Your main reason for visiting Celbridge, however, is to see Castletown House, reputedly the largest private house in Ireland. By the mid-1960s it was almost derelict, and it was then that Desmond Guinness bought it and, with the aid of the Irish Georgian Society of which he was president until 1992, began an extensive restoration programme. When I first saw the house in 1967 it was still in a dire state, thieves having stolen much of the lead from the roof, but the transformation has been remarkable.

An early Georgian mansion, built about 1722, its owner was William Conolly, Speaker of the Irish House of Commons and the country's first millionaire. Originally a tavern-keeper's son from Donegal, Conolly became a lawyer and grew rich by creaming off commissions when Irish lands were, once again, being redistributed following the Williamite Revolution. The front of the house, which is a trifle austere, was designed in the style of a sixteenth-century Italian town palace and rises to an imposing 60 feet. It is joined by semicircular colonnades to two gracious pavilions, one on each side, giving a 400-foot frontage altogether. The original architect was indeed an Italian, Alessandro Galilei (who later designed the façade of St John Lateran in Rome, no less) but others had a hand in the finished work, notably Sir Edward Lovett Pearce, principal architect of the Parliament House in Dublin. The entrance hall is an imposing two-storeyed room with a black and white chequered floor and was designed by Pearce. The Ionic order on the lower storey matches the colonnades outside, and at gallery

---

Lord Wavertree had this garden in Co. Kildare laid out in the Japanese style in 1906, complete with a Gate of Oblivion and Hill of Ambition.

level there are pilasters with baskets of flowers and fruit carved in wood. The staircase is magnificent, a cantilevered affair in Portland stone with superb brass banisters (the delicate stucco work on the walls is by the Francinis) rising to a Long Gallery decorated in the Pompeian manner by Charles Reuben Riley and Thomas Ryder, a pupil of Reynolds. The gallery, 80 feet long by 23 feet wide, is a spectacular sight, with four large sheets of mirrored French glass on the walls, busts of poets and philosophers on gilded brackets, a seventeenth-century statue of Diana tucked in a central niche and three magnificent Murano glass chandeliers whose blue, alas, does not quite match the walls. In the 1770s, when the gallery was used as the family living room, it was filled with exquisite furniture, and card-parties and other activities were enjoyed here. The house is only partially furnished nowadays, with whatever appropriate objects the Georgian Society and the Castletown Foundation, set up by Desmond Guinness in 1979, have been able to obtain, but oddly enough the relative emptiness somehow enhances the magnificence of the house itself.

A relaxed drive along the main Dublin–Cork road will bring you to two centres of considerable importance to the Irish story. The first is The Curragh, twelve square miles of unfenced land, part of which was once the headquarters of the British army in Ireland, the rest the site of the famous racecourse (where chariots were raced two thousand years ago). The second is the town of Kildare where St Brigid, honoured as the 'Virgin of the Gael', founded her famous monastery in the sixth century. The military part of The Curragh was the scene of the notorious 1914 'mutiny' when General Hubert Gough, later commander of the 5th Army in France, and other officers indicated that they would resign rather than march on Belfast to 'coerce' the Unionists and Orange-

men into obeying the Irish Home Rule Act which had already been passed by Parliament. The racecourse itself may have lost a certain chic with the disappearance of the English officery and the Ascendancy but meetings here are still fashionable events by the standards of Ireland's sturdy democracy.

The town of Kildare exudes an ineradicable, almost tangible, atmosphere of horsiness rather than sanctity, which is no more than one might expect from its situation in the heart of Ireland's Newmarket or Kentucky Blue Grass country, with the National Stud and other outstanding stud farms ringing the vicinity. The cathedral of St Brigid was founded in 1229 but is now almost totally a work of restoration, though it has a fine 106-foot round tower – in this case lacking the familiar and proper cone top. The reverence for St Brigid remains an ambiguous matter, containing as it does strong pagan elements. The very name Brigid derives from the daughter of the Dagda, who was chief of the old Celtic gods and was also worshipped by the Celts of Britain and Gaul. Brigid, in her various forms, Brigantia, Brid and so on, was a goddess of fire and, indeed, a flame was kept burning perpetually in the monastery here from its foundation until the Dissolution under Henry VIII.

A mile to the south-east of the town lies the National Stud, which is open to visitors, but if your interest in horses is limited the adjoining Japanese Gardens are well worth visiting. They were laid out in 1906 by a Japanese called Eito for Lord Wavertree and you can pass happily through the Gate of Oblivion and the Garden of Temptation, ascend the Hill of Ambition and visit a Geisha House (alas, without any geishas, however) all within an hour of St Stephen's Green.

On your way back to Dublin, if your imagination has been lit by some of the old Celtic tales of Ireland, you may feel inclined to make a slight detour to see the Hill of Allen. This was the legendary stronghold of the great champion Finn MacCool and his warrior company, the Fianna – each man of which took an oath never to flee before fewer than ten enemies. Almost a thousand years before the concept of chivalry imbued medieval knighthood, the Fianna practised its

---

St Laurence's Gate, one of Drogheda's medieval town gates. It escaped destruction by Cromwell in a ferocious massacre when almost the entire population was slain.

principles, the purpose of their existence being to protect women, uphold honour, punish wickedness and, in general, preserve Ireland against her enemies.

From Dublin you should now head directly north along the spacious, if uneven and juggernaut-infested, main road to Drogheda and into the heartland of ancient Ireland. The very name Drogheda (Drock-eh-da) still carries a chilling connotation for every Catholic Irishman, for it was here that Cromwell and his parliamentarians, in a vehement anti-Catholic outburst, committed what historians generally agree was one of the worst atrocities ever perpetrated in the British Isles. The town, rising steeply on each side of the River Boyne, had been an important site since 911 when the Vikings first fortified it; later the Normans built it into one of the country's principal towns, with a right to conduct a university (never exercised). When Cromwell arrived in the country in 1649 Drogheda was in the hands of Royalists, most of them, ironically, Englishmen. The great man, it should be noted, had an intense pecuniary interest in the Irish campaign for he had a large stake in an enterprise set up under an Adventurers' Act whose objective was to exploit Irish land after it had been seized. He almost certainly believed that the Protestant settlers of Ulster had been the victims of a horrendous massacre during the 1641 Irish Rebellion when the native Catholics, cheated of their lands and rights by the Jacobean Plantation of Ulster, wreaked revenge on the newcomers. Horrors, it has to be said, did occur, but the alleged figure of ten thousand murders was wildly exaggerated by propaganda. Cromwell chose Drogheda as his first target but had to fight hard for victory, managing to succeed only on the third assault, which may have incensed him even further. Whatever the cause of his action, he ordered the death of all the defenders, and almost three thousand people were massacred – in effect, the entire population. When a hundred people managed to reach the sanctuary of the steeple of St Peter's Church, he ordered the place burned down, hailing the screams of the victims as 'a marvellous great mercy'. The gaunt shell of that steeple still stands.

Drogheda today has become a bustling town of narrow, car-jammed streets. Luckily, it also possesses the remains of two fine thirteenth-century town gates, Butter Gate and St Laurence's Gate, the latter a picturesque edifice of two tall drum towers linked by a loop-holed curtain, part of the ancient barbican. Drogheda's most gruesome relic is the embalmed head of St Oliver Plunkett, a seventeenth-century Archbishop of Armagh who, in yet another fit of English anti-Catholicism, was hanged, drawn and quartered at Tyburn on a trumped-up charge; his head is now kept in a glass case in a side altar of St Peter's Catholic Church.

From Drogheda you can embark on a glorious tour of the sylvan Boyne Valley. First, though, I suggest you drive to the ancient monastic site of Monasterboice, which has two of the finest high crosses in the country. The earlier and best preserved is Muireadach's Cross, one side of which depicts scenes from the New Testament, the other the Old. The West Cross is among the tallest ever raised anywhere in Ireland, standing almost 22 feet high, but it has deteriorated badly. These high crosses began as simple wooden crosses, then evolved into stone monoliths and finally were used to carry carvings picked out in glowing paint, which were literally 'sermons in stone' for a largely illiterate population. The typical Celtic ring around the centre of these crosses was intended originally as a simple support for the heavy arms but was later developed to symbolize the cosmos, which had as its central event the Crucifixion. Also at Monasterboice are the ruins of two churches, one dating from the thirteenth century, the other slightly earlier, an ancient sundial and a round tower which, despite being shorn of its apex, is still over 100 feet high.

You are now only three miles from Mellifont, which provides a beautiful setting for the tranquil ruins of a

The early tenth-century Muireadach's Cross at Monasterboice, near the River Boyne. Its deeply incised panels depict biblical scenes.

great Cistercian monastery that played an important role in Irish ecclesiastical history. St Malachy, a former Archbishop of Armagh, was one of the great twelfth-century 'reformers' who were intent on sweeping away the immorality, corruption and nepotism which had disfigured the Irish Church at this time, and to bring its practices into line with Rome. He visited his friend St Bernard of Clairvaux, and was so impressed by the rule there that he had some Irish novices trained at Clairvaux; accompanied by a party of French Cistercians, they arrived in Mellifont in 1142. Soon daughter establishments were flourishing in other parts of Ireland. At the consecration of the first church here, Dervorgilla, whose elopement with Dermot MacMurrough, the king of Leinster, was to bring about the Norman conquest of Ireland, presented the foundation with sixty ounces of gold, a gold chalice and other ornaments. After her stormy affair with MacMurrough, she eventually retired here and stayed until her death. Following the Dissolution, the abbey buildings passed into the hands of the Moore family, ancestors of the earls of Drogheda, who turned them into a fortified residence. It was from this house that Hugh O'Neill, Earl of Tyrone, last and greatest of Gaelic chieftains, starved into surrender after the disastrous Battle of Kinsale, finally submitted to the English Crown and brought to an end a social and political system that had endured for almost two thousand years. It is, indeed, a haunted place.

You are now within reach of yet another evocative place – this time what is perhaps the most sacred portion of turf in the world for the Orangemen of Northern Ireland and their kindred in Scotland, Canada and other places where they have scattered; the site of the Battle of the Boyne, which was fought here on 1 July (according to the old calendar) 1690 between William of Orange and James II. In 1689 James had landed at Kinsale from France with a contingent of French troops and with money supplied by Louis XIV, whose strategic plan for Europe included the restoration of his client James to the British throne. Himself a convert to the old faith, James was deeply conscious of the undoubted injustices that had

been perpetrated upon Irish Catholics by Cromwell, and of the efforts of his brother, Charles II, to rectify them. His first act on reaching Dublin, therefore, was to call a parliament which restored certain Catholic rights, but it also had the effect of stirring Irish Protestants to fury. When he attempted to seize Derry, the 'Apprentice Boys of Derry' shut the gates against him and his siege ended in failure. By this time, William, alert to the dangers threatening the 'Glorious Revolution', quickly crossed to Ireland, landing at Carrickfergus on Belfast Lough with a highly professional army of thirty-six thousand men, which was joined by some Huguenots who had settled in Ulster and other Protestant settlers. James by this time had withdrawn to the south side of the Boyne with an army of seven thousand French and some eighteen thousand Irish Catholic farmers, few of whom had ever fired a blunderbuss in their lives.

The battle, which began at dawn, was decided when William sent a force of ten thousand men westwards towards Rosnaree and Slane with the idea of outflanking James's forces on their left. By 10.30 am he and his main forces were ready to cross the Boyne as the outflanking movement began to sweep up the Jacobite army. A bridge near Oldbridge now marks the spot where he crossed, not without difficulty, however, as he was almost unhorsed; worse, his general, Marshal Schomberg, who had fought with him against Louis XIV in many great Continental battles, had his head carried off. In the end, despite several dashing charges by the Irish cavalry led by Patrick Sarsfield (who was to die on the field of Landen, fighting for the French and declaring, 'Would that this were for Ireland!'), the Jacobites were routed; James fled to Dublin and thence to France. Over the next century Irish Catholics were to suffer more grievously than ever from harsh penal laws which made them little better than out-

---

Oldbridge, on the River Boyne, was the site of a decisive victory for William of Orange over James II, which decided Ireland's fate for the next three centuries.

casts and serfs in their own country. For the Protestants of Ulster it was a most blessed deliverance from popery – a fact they have not forgotten to this day.

A short distance upstream, in a beautifully wooded bend of the river, lies a two-mile stretch of country known as Brugh-na-Boinne (The Palace of the Boyne), which might be loosely described as an Irish Valley of the Kings. Here are some of the richest and most haunted prehistoric remains in Europe, a vast necropolis of passage graves used for the burial of pagan kings, priests and eminent men since the Stone Age, and later sacred to Celtic gods such as Dagda, Aengus and Boinne. Newgrange, the only excavated tumulus as yet open to the public, is believed to be just under 5500 years old. There are three great tumuli in Brugh-na-Boinne, the other two being Knowth and Dowth, as well as literally dozens of mounds, rises and hills and at least twenty great passage graves. Knowth is even more complex in both construction and range of decoration than Newgrange, while Dowth is known to be larger and even older, almost certainly the oldest man-made structure in Europe.

The exterior of Newgrange has been magnificently reconstructed, using the original white quartz stones found lying about on the site. Covering an area of over an acre, standing 44 feet high and comprising more than two hundred thousand tons of rock, the monument presents a dazzling white spectacle that can be seen for miles; a strikingly graceful bow-fronted structure set on a high ridge, it could easily be mistaken for a space ship. The entrance is guarded by a huge stone engraved with triple spirals which immediately seize your imagination; what can they mean? The passageway itself is narrow, the sides consisting of enormous slabs of stone emblazoned with spirals, lozenges, curves and rectangles. The passageway runs exactly 62 feet from the entrance to the central

Among the oldest man-made structures in Europe, Newgrange predates Stonehenge by 1500 years. It was an important religious and burial site.

chamber, which is an awe-inspiring room, corbelled to a height of 19 feet and stretching 10 feet across, with stones decorated with zigzags, coils, triangles, and other shapes in a dazzling display of abstract art that in its time was not equalled elsewhere. Let into the walls are three recesses with stone troughs where it is thought the cremated remains of the dead were laid, with trinkets and offerings, as in Egyptian tombs.

The most stunning aspect of Newgrange and possibly its greatest mystery is a small opening set above the doorway, now called the 'roof box'. In 1849 Sir William Wilde, Oscar's father, a noted antiquarian as well as an eminent medical man, was working on the site when he prised away a small flat stone; at first he thought it merely marked the entrance to another passage. Then at the dawn of the winter solstice, 21 December, he discovered that the sun's rays shone directly through this aperture, illuminating the central chamber with a great golden light for a full seventeen minutes. This meant that Newgrange was one of the earliest structures ever built in alignment with the sun. Still more astonishing is the fact that this level of precision, allowing for changes in the earth's angle to the sun over a period of five thousand years, would be almost impossible to achieve even with our own advanced technology today. Apart from the tumuli, there are also a considerable number of artefacts dating from the Stone and Bronze Ages nearby, as well as the remains of a settlement of Beaker folk; the most impressive of these Beaker remains are the Great Circle of twelve huge stones in front of Newgrange and, not far away, relics of an enormous circle of wooden posts, the largest structure of its type in the world.

Leaving Newgrange, your drive takes you through the quiet, lush countryside of Royal Meath, with its many superb private estates; almost none of them, sadly, are open to the public but they add richness to an often bedraggled landscape. The village of Slane was built by the Conynham family as a manorial village, with four fine Georgian houses on each corner of the crossroads at the centre. The Hill of Slane has gained its fame as the alleged site where St Patrick lit his Paschal Fire in AD 433 to herald the arrival of

Christianity to the high king of Tara. Under druidic law, such fires were forbidden, and Patrick was hauled before King Laoghaire to explain himself. Laoghaire listened to the saint and, though he refused to accept the new faith himself, gave Patrick leave to continue his mission. The views from the summit of Slane Hill are worth the gentle climb, with vistas extending south as far as the Sugar Loaf and north to the hills around Dundalk, near the Northern Irish border. The ruins on the summit are of a Franciscan friary said to be built upon an earlier church founded by St Erc, one of Patrick's converts.

Navan has little to commend it, despite its choice situation at the confluence of the Blackwater and Boyne rivers, which is dispiriting because it was here that Heremon, son of Miles, leader of the Celts who invaded Ireland, decided to abandon his wife and marry Tea, daughter of a local prince, whose name lives on in history through Tara (Tea Mur, meaning Tea's fort). It deserves something better.

There is a great deal to divert your interest as you traverse this area, for the relics of history press hard on each other. Kells is a relatively neat town, where the great Book (see p. 39) was kept for many centuries and where Columcille's House, occupied by the monks of Iona when they fled to Ireland after the sack of their mother-foundation by Vikings, is worth a quick viewing. On the summit of the nearby Loughcrew Hills is yet another astounding necropolis of passage graves, mounds, megaliths and ring forts dating from 2000 BC.

Trim demands attention because it was here that the largest stone castle ever built in Ireland was raised by the Normans. As it is, the walls, eleven feet thick at their most solid, and what remains of its towers, extend over nearly three acres. The castle began its existence as a motte and bailey in 1173; it was constructed by Hugh de Lacy who had half a million acres of Meath to play with, having been made Viceroy by Henry II, but it was levelled the following year by Rory O'Connor, Ireland's last high king. In 1210 it was again rebuilt to house King John (since when it has been known as King John's Castle), who wanted to show the De Lacys that they were not independent princes, however powerful they thought they were, but he gave it back to them in 1215. The great keep, with a tower 75 feet high, was built in two stages by Walter de Lacy and Geoffrey de Grenville, who spent many years on the Crusades (his brother, Jean, was the constant companion and biographer of St Louis, king of France). The most impressive part of the remains is the Dublin Gate, which has a massive barbican and two drawbridges, each with a portcullis; it was in the tower above the gate that Prince Hal of Lancaster, later King Henry V, was imprisoned by Richard II in 1399. Several Anglo-Norman parliaments were held here throughout the next century, an enactment of the 1447 Parliament being that any man who wished to be accepted as English had to abandon his Irish-style moustache and shave both lips.

In the same village, on the ruins of a castle built by Sir John Talbot (who got the worst of it when he faced Joan of Arc at Orleans), was a Protestant school where the Duke of Wellington was once a pupil. The town itself raised a column in his honour in 1815, and even though Ireland is no longer dependent (politically) on Britain, his name is still revered as a fellow townsman.

Take your leave of Trim travelling east by the R154 and turn north towards Kilmessan; within a mile or so you reach the most famous site in all Ireland – Tara.

Tara of the Kings is one of the bedrocks of the Irish imagination, of Irish culture, of Irish history. It is as precious and significant to Ireland as Athens is to Greece, and the Celtic tales which have Tara as their centre are an Irish *Iliad*. Here is a sacral site over four thousand years old which gradually evolved into the seat of the high kings and priests of Tara; as Gaelic Ireland fought a tortuous way towards a centralized monarchy – taking its ideas from Rome and establishing its dominion long before England and France fought the Hundred Years War – Tara became the seat

The Norman castle at Trim, Co. Meath. In the tower shown here, Hal of Lancaster, later Henry V of England, was imprisoned by Richard II in 1399.

Tara, a 5000-year-old sacral site where the ancient High Kings of Ireland reigned, remains a powerful symbol of Celtic Ireland.

of the high kings of Ireland and of Celtic majesty. In short, it is the Irish Camelot – in fact much of the Arthurian cycle, including the legend of Excalibur, derives from these ancient Irish sagas.

Oddly enough, for all its fame and the aura of romance surrounding its name, the Hill of Tara is not a particularly spectacular site. In Britain, for instance, Maiden Castle in Dorset, British Camp in the Malverns and many other Iron Age remains, built as impregnable fortresses on craggy eminences, appear far more dramatic. Most of Ireland's kingly sites, however, are pitched on relatively low, gentle hills, easy of access. This, I think, is probably because they all originally had a religious purpose. Indeed, Tara itself appears to have begun as a Neolithic passage grave (it has been dated to 2100 BC) while the body of a boy was found in a later grave, dating from 1350 BC, with, interestingly, faience beads from Egypt beside him.

The site became of real significance in Irish history in the third century AD, when King Cormac MacArt constructed most of the impressive buildings that, according to tradition, once stood on this site. These were, of course, mainly built of mud and wattle and have long since rotted away to earthen humps, but descriptions, perhaps fanciful, perhaps true enough, have come down to us. Certainly the outline of what appears to have been a banqueting hall can still be seen (although some archaeologists argue that it was simply a processional way – similar perhaps to the Avenue of Rams leading to the Temple of Khonsu at Thebes). It covers an area measuring 750 feet by 90 feet and here, it is said, up to a thousand people were entertained during the great *feis* of Samhain, marking both the end of summer and the feast of the dead. The building was said to have had five aisles, 'the central a circulation passage with hearths, cauldrons, torches and so on, the others divided into booths or cubicles allocated according to social precedence'. It was undoubtedly this great hall, which historical sources tell us had doors inset with precious stones and furnishings of gold and bronze, that Thomas Moore was thinking of when he penned his famous song, which can still stir the hearts of Irishmen:

The harp that once through Tara's halls,
The soul of music shed,
Now hangs as mute on Tara's walls,
As if that soul were fled,
So sleeps the pride of former days . . .

The central area of the complex, the Rath of the Kings, is limited by a great earthen rampart, inside which are two smaller circular earthworks named Cormac's House and the Royal Seat. To the north is the Mound of the Hostages, covering the early passage grave. Near here lay a fallen pillar stone (now removed to the Rath of the Kings) which is alleged to be the Lia Fail, the Stone of Destiny. The stone belongs to Tara all right, but it actually stands today as a commemoration of the 1798 rebels.

A stone of destiny did, indeed, once rest at Tara. This stone, upon which the kings stood to be acclaimed (it was supposed to give a roar of approval if the rightful king were crowned), was said to be the pillow on which Jacob dreamed of ascending a ladder to heaven. When Nebuchadnezzar destroyed the Temple in Jerusalem, the legend goes that a party of Israelites fled to Ireland, taking 'the pillow' with them – a far-fetched tale obviously used as a propaganda weapon when Christianity was fighting to establish itself over paganism in Ireland. So strong was the belief in it, however, that in the 1880s a party of zealous British Israelites vandalized the Rath of the Synods in a vain search for the Ark of the Covenant.

As for the stone of destiny, history records that Muircheatach I sent the original Tara stone to the Scotti (Irish Celts), who had founded the kingdom of Dalriada in Argyll, to ensure that a 'king of the Scotti' would always rule there. It was kept in the castle of Dunstaffnage until the union of Scots and Picts under King Kenneth MacAlpin created a new united kingdom of Scotland, when Kenneth removed it to Scone, the old capital of the Picts. Here it remained until seized by Edward I and brought to Westminster, where it sits under the throne of British monarchs at their coronation. The great mystery, of course, is whether this stone is the original Lia Fail or not, for it is not Irish or even Palestinian stone but Scottish, suggesting that it was substituted at some stage for the original. It is quite possible, of course, that the genuine Lia Fail was returned to Ireland after it had served its purpose in Dalriada and that what we see at Tara is, indeed, the original stone of destiny. Certainly the only proper place for it is here, in this place so redolent of all that symbolizes the land and people of Celtic Ireland.

2
Wexford and the Invasion Route

Wexford – Enniscorthy – Avoca – Avondale – Kilkenny

Inistioge – Carrick-on-Suir – Clonmel – Lismore

Ardmore – Waterford

The conventional image of Ireland – of luminescent lakes, blue mountains, rock-strewn fields, bogs dark as *sachertorte*, and peasant cottages coated in generations of whitewash – simply does not hold here. This south-eastern corner of the country is quite distinctive, due partly to topography and partly to the confluence of different ethnic groups and cultures. Most of Co. Wexford was inhabited in Christ's time by the Brigantes, a British Celtic tribe who also held northern England. North of these were the Corionii and north again, stretching up into what is now north Wicklow and south Dublin, the Menapii, a tribe of Belgae from the Meuse and lower Rhine who fled to Ireland to escape Caesar's legions. So already we have the beginnings of an ethnic hotchpotch. Add to these, then, the Gaelic Celts who arrived some time in the first century AD, the Norse who founded the town of Wexford (they called it Weissfjord) in the ninth century, the all-conquering Normans in the twelfth and the Cromwellians, who turned it into a garrison town in the seventeenth and we have, indeed, a full-blooded Irish stew, bubbling and boiling with a rich assortment of cultural influences. As late as the start of the twentieth century, three different languages were

being spoken here – Irish, English and Yola, which is a mixture of Flemish, old Norman-English and old Saxon. The region's varied inheritance is further emphasized by the gamut of names of the people who live here: Kinsella, Murphy, Doran, Hayes, Keohoe, Nolan, O'Connor, Larkin, Doyle, Sweetman, Dake, Fleming, Sinnott, Roche, Prendergast, Pender, Walsh, Wallace, Devereux, French, Lambert, Power (la Poer), Neville, Rossiter, Furlong, Harvey, Etchingham, Millar, Browne, Moore, Jenkins, Hamilton, Hempenstall. There is also a recent and growing influx of German, Italian and oriental patronymics.

People, landscape, climate, all show a marked diversity from the rest of the country. This is the driest and warmest part of Ireland, temperatures reaching an average of 62 degrees Fahrenheit in high summer. Its eastern littoral, unlike any other part of the country, consists of an unbroken stretch of some thirty miles of low-lying land fringed by largely deserted beaches of fine sand, normally ignored by those who prefer stark theatre in their landscape. As you move inland you find undulating pastures, festoons of effusive woodland and placid river valleys of a quiet beauty that makes you wonder if this is really Ireland at all. For the

rest it is a region of sea inlets and tranquil creeks, dozy little fishing harbours, portal dolmens and Celtic raths, ruined medieval abbeys, fortresses, castles and a couple of nineteenth-century masterpieces by Augustus Welby Pugin. It also provides a broad and unique seam in the texture of the Irish story, for great – and horrible – events occurred in this area. Cromwell, for example, repeated his Drogheda atrocities at Wexford town, putting the entire garrison of fifteen hundred men to the sword and routing out and massacring every last priest that could be found. Nor were women and children exempted. It was an effective policy, of course, for many Irish towns which had planned to resist him caved in without firing a shot.

You may find Wexford town disappointing, although its shape – it is only a third as wide as it is long – and its attenuated quays have a certain appeal. The Slaney river empties here and over the centuries has silted up much of the harbour, which scarcely lends enchantment. The quays themselves, although spacious enough, are not garnished with any meritorious buildings, and perhaps the only object worth looking at is a statue – a gift from the US Government – to Commodore John Barry, 'Father of the US Navy', who was born a few miles away. Barry was responsible for commissioning the first Continental fleet and fought many daring and successful actions against the British; he was also chosen to command the ship carrying Lafayette back to France after Yorktown and ended his career tutoring many of the men who were eventually to command the US Navy.

Interest should quicken as you begin exploring the alleyways and narrow streets that lead up from the quays to the long, curving main street; just before it you reach the Bull Ring, which saw at least three hundred years of bull-baiting, ending only in 1792; it was here too that Cromwell's pikemen slaughtered

Wexford, one of the first urban settlements in Ireland, was founded by Vikings, and its streets still follow the original plan.

three hundred Wexford women as they knelt in the roadway begging for mercy in 1649. But frankly, there is not all that much to see in the town; the Thomas Moore Tavern is where the poet's mother was born; Robert McClure, discoverer of the North-West Passage, was born in a house now incorporated in White's Hotel and just opposite lived Michael Balfe, composer of *The Bohemian Girl* and a score of other operas.

There is, however, Westgate, dating from the fourteenth century, the only one of the town's six medieval gates still remaining, and there are remnants of the town walls. Wexford's most interesting relic is Selskar (Holy Sepulchre) Abbey nearby, where Henry II did penance for Becket's murder and where he signed the first Anglo-Irish Treaty. Three miles to the east of the town is the area rather quaintly known as The Slobs, mud flats sheltering behind the sea walls of the Slaney estuary. A noted wildfowl reserve, the Slobs are the wintering ground for some fifty per cent of the world's Greenland white-fronted geese, but there are also Bewick's swans, blacktailed godwits, pintails, gulls, terns and redshanks to be seen here.

Every October the town is taken over by music lovers, who amble forth from White's Hotel in evening dress, stroll through narrow streets originally laid out to accommodate horn-helmeted Vikings, and crowd into a tiny eighteenth-century theatre to listen to long-forgotten arias by Boieldieu or Donizetti, sung by some of the finest bel canto voices in the world. This is the internationally famous Wexford Opera Festival, a long way from the culture of boiled potatoes and buttermilk that is so often associated with bucolic Ireland.

Wexford sets a high gastronomic standard, and its seafood offerings are among the finest anywhere: oysters, mussels, whelks, trout and salmon are all magnificent, while the local smoked salmon is the most delicious I have ever tasted. During festival time it has become almost obligatory to take a lunchtime cruise up the River Barrow on a floating restaurant which provides superb food as well as glorious vistas of autumnal colours.

It is history, of course, that makes Wexford, town and county, of stirring significance to the Irish story:

We are the boys of Wexford
Who fought with heart and hand
To burst in twain the galling chain,
And free our native land!

In 1798 Ireland was – not unusually by any means – in turmoil, and the authorities were in a state of near panic concerning the involvement of revolutionary France, where the radical Irishman Theobald Wolfe Tone had been trying to persuade the Directory to liberate Ireland. In December 1796 a French fleet anchored in Bantry Bay, but it ran into atrocious weather and found it impossible to land its fifteen thousand soldiers. In 1797 a combined Franco-Dutch fleet with fourteen thousand soldiers aboard was intercepted at Camperdown by the British. But disorder was already widespread throughout Ireland, affecting even the staunch Protestants of Ulster. Flogging, burning, torture, shooting or hanging had become a fate that anyone, even the innocent, might suffer at the hands of troops and militia who, apparently out of control, roamed the country. The leaders of the United Irishmen, a revolutionary organization (and the origin of the modern republican movement), planned a rising for 23 May 1798. Spies tipped off the Government who arrested and executed the leaders, but a rising, nonetheless, broke out. No one expected it to explode where it did, in Co. Wexford, where so many of the population were Old English, but it was they in the end who proved the most determined rebels.

The insurrection began in the hamlet of Boolavogue, near Enniscorthy, on 26 May when some dragoons abused local people walking on the road. Father John Murphy, the local parish priest, was so incensed that he sent out a call to arms. The response was a force of pikemen and a hundred or so men who could use a musket. Murphy turned out to be a superb commander, inflicting a series of defeats on the bodies of troops initially sent to oppose him, and as more rebels joined the cause he and his men seized Enniscorthy and then Wexford town, eventually controlling most of the county. Strategically, the rebels had to break out of the region to raise the rest of the country, but although they seized Gorey, opening the way to Dublin, they failed to exploit their advantage. The greatest fighting of the campaign actually took place at New Ross where ten thousand rebels, armed only with pikes, under the command of Bagenal Harvey, a Protestant landowner, attacked the garrison of fourteen hundred men. It proved the stuff of true melodrama: charge after furious charge was repulsed until eventually sheer persistence and courage won the day, but the victorious rebels gave themselves over to plunder and drunken celebration, allowing the troops to rally and eject them with bloody loss.

The rising, which might have given Ireland her independence 120 years before it was eventually achieved, and without the problems that partition of the country has brought, sadly degenerated into a series of sickening atrocities. Catholic resentments were intense after all that the country had undergone since the Elizabethan re-conquest, and particularly after a century of viciously anti-Catholic penal laws. Protestants who supported the Government were treated abominably; a common death was to stick a couple of pikes through a man's chest or belly and another couple through his back, then hoist him high and hang him there until he expired. When the rebellion collapsed, troops and militia proved equally barbaric, a favourite torture being to pour tar over a captive's head and set it alight. Nor was it an uncommon sight to see the heads of dead rebels being kicked around the streets of Wexford by troops in macabre games of football.

Enniscorthy, fourteen miles north of Wexford, is a presentable town boasting a statue to Father Murphy in its market place. Its fine museum, whose collection consists mainly of relics from the rising of '98, is housed in the Norman castle that dominates the town. The castle itself, once the home of the poet Spenser, is

The ruins of the medieval Selskar Abbey, Wexford. Here Henry II signed the Treaty of Windsor which laid down the conditions of English overlordship.

worth inspection. The Catholic cathedral, St Aidan's, is by Pugin, and is considered one of the best examples in Ireland of the Gothic Revival style. Arguably the town's greatest claim to fame, though, is the 391-foot hill on its outskirts; this is Vinegar Hill, where the '98 rebels had their principal encampment. Their command post was in a windmill of which nothing but the stump remains. Here, on 21 June, they made their last stand, besieged by twenty thousand troops under the command of General Lake who bombarded them with incessant artillery fire. Although the rebels were also numerous they had little but pikes with which to fight. Nevertheless, they withstood the bombardment throughout the day until darkness allowed some of them to escape. Father Murphy led this remnant towards Kilkenny, hoping to raise fresh support, but they were surrounded and he was taken to Tullow, Co. Carlow, where he was hanged.

Ferns, seven miles to the north of Enniscorthy, is not much more than a village nowadays, yet it is one of the pivotal sites of Irish history. In the twelfth century this was the capital of Leinster whose king, Dermot MacMurrough, has become the most execrated of all Irishmen, a national traitor, the man who brought the Normans to Ireland and with them English domination for almost eight hundred years. The town's history begins in the sixth century with the foundation of a monastery by St Aidan, whose remains lie enshrined in a casket in the National Museum in Dublin. The ruins in Ferns are impressive. The castle, of Norman-Irish type – a rectangular keep with drum towers at the corners – was Dermot's headquarters. At the other end of the village are the remains of an early thirteenth century cathedral now incorporated into a small nineteenth-century Church of Ireland cathedral. South of this stands St Mary's Abbey, founded by Dermot for Canons Regular of St Augustine, the only remains of

With its twin thirteenth-century towers and curtain walls still standing, the remains of Ferns Castle, Co. Wexford, are still impressive.

Designed by A. W. Pugin, the cathedral at Enniscorthy, Co. Wexford, is considered one of Ireland's best examples of Gothic Revival architecture.

which are a vaulted sacristy, the 64-foot long wall of a nave-and-chancel church and an extraordinary ruined belfry, which rises as a square tower to the level of the church roof and is then suddenly transformed into a round bell-tower. In the nearby graveyard do stop and examine the stump of a high cross which, at some time, appears to have been vandalized – understandably, I should have thought, as this is the grave of Dermot MacMurrough.

The Irish version of history, at least, cannot see Dermot as other than a villain, a man whose inability to control his stormy passions was to bring centuries of ruin to his country. He was the product of ambiguous times. A tall, handsome man, Dermot was highly cultured and a noted patron of art and religion. In his library he kept one of the glories of Irish literature, the Book of Leinster, a marvellous compilation of history and literature which he had commissioned. He founded many monasteries and churches and richly endowed All Saints in Dublin as well as magnificent Jerpoint Abbey in Kilkenny. Yet he was totally ruthless. It must be admitted that he needed to be if he and his kingdom were to survive; it was only by hard fighting that he became king of Leinster at all, having to subdue several rival Gaelic lords and force the Dublin Norse to recognize his authority. He dealt harshly with any opposition; when a number of chieftains revolted against him in 1141 he personally blinded or slew some seventeen of them after he had quelled their revolt. When he wanted a woman relative made Abbess of Kildare he disposed of the incumbent by ordering one of his common soldiers to rape her, thus rendering her unfit for continued office. Then, in 1152, he committed his big mistake. On a visit to Dromahair, seat of Tiernan O'Rourke, Lord of Breffni, he decided to carry off the latter's wife, Dervorgilla. The lady may well have been willing, for O'Rourke was no oil painting while Dermot could turn any woman's head. In the end, of course, after she had borne him a child, he deserted her and she retired to Mellifont Abbey for the rest of her days. O'Rourke, however, never forgave Dermot and in 1166 headed a combined force which routed him.

A lesser mortal might have simply knuckled under. Instead, Dermot fled to Bristol where he was advised to travel to France and seek assistance from Henry II. It may be supposed that he was aware that Henry had in his possession a papal bull ('Laudabiliter'), giving him the pope's authority to invade Ireland to reform the Irish Church. This authority was based on a document ('The Donation of Constantine') which purported to subject all Christian islands to the pope's jurisdiction — a document which later turned out to be a forgery. Henry, however, had been dissuaded from putting the

bull into operation by his mother, the Empress Matilda, who argued that Ireland was 'holy ground'. Despite Dermot's pleas, therefore, Henry refused his personal help but finally agreed to allow Dermot to recruit any helpers he could find within Norman dominions. Dermot returned to Bristol but had little luck until an impoverished knight called Richard FitzGilbert de Clare approached him. To enlist his aid, Dermot promised De Clare, known to history as Strongbow, his daughter in marriage and succession to his kingdom of Leinster. This stirred other Norman knights to volunteer, among them Strongbow's cousin, Maurice Fitzgerald, who was to found the Geraldine dynasty (later ennobled as earls of Kildare and dukes of Leinster), among the greatest of all Anglo-Irish families. Dermot returned to Ireland and with the backing of a small group of Flemish mercenaries managed to survive in south Leinster. On 1 May 1169 an advance party of Strongbow's forces landed at Bannow Bay, Co. Wexford, followed by a second party the next day. Employing the long bow and mailed cavalry, a combination which the Irish had never encountered before, they seized Wexford town. In May 1170, in response to desperate pleas from a force about to be thrown out of Ireland, another group of Normans arrived at Baginbun; finally, on 23 August, Strongbow himself landed near Crooke, just outside Waterford. He took Waterford in bloody attack, married Dermot's daughter Eva as the town streets ran with blood, and within a month controlled all Leinster. This was the start of the Norman Conquest.

We continue northwards now, towards Co. Wicklow, with the fine outline of the 2610-foot-high Mount Leinster (where the last wolf in Ireland was killed), peak of the Blackstairs chain, slowly fading away to the left. Gorey is scarcely worth more than a pause for refreshment and you might care, instead, to turn

---

Charles Stewart Parnell walked these woodlands on his estate in Avondale as he pondered the campaign which eventually abolished feudalism in Ireland.

This dolmen at Browne's Hill, Co. Carlow, is the largest in Ireland and almost certainly in Europe. The capstone measures 5 ft thick and weighs over 100 tons.

sharply right and make for the coast, where the small harbour of Courtown will give you access to an excellent two-mile beach. Before reaching Arklow you will see on your right a signpost marked Tara Hill. This is not, of course, *the* Tara but an 853-foot hill giving excellent views over the rather flat countryside around. Back on the main road again, continue to Arklow which, despite its stormy history, has little to detain you. It was sacked in 1315 by Edward Bruce, Robert's brother, whom the Ulster Irish had accepted as their king; with his brother's help, Edward hoped to turn the English out of Ireland altogether and make himself the new high king. Cromwell passed through here, too, putting the place in order, and finally in 1798, led by another Father Murphy, an army of insurgents, armed only with pitchforks, attempted to seize the town.

We are now back into superb Co. Wicklow, in the Vale of Avoca, where a pretty stretch of water runs between wooded banks – a spot the Victorians considered one of the most delightful in Ireland. It is said to be what he saw here that led the poet Thomas Moore to write the famous lines:

> There is not in the wide world a valley so sweet,
> As the vale in whose bosom the bright waters meet. . . .
> Sweet Vale of Avoca, how calm could I rest
> In thy bosom of shade with the friends I love best,
> Where the storms that we feel in this cold world
>   should cease,
> And our hearts, like thy waters, be mingled in peace.

But where exactly did the waters meet? Woodenbridge, where the river Aughrim meets the Avoca, claims that this is where Moore found his inspiration. It is, indeed, a handsome enough place, gentle and well-wooded and relatively peaceful. Others argue that Moore's inspiration arose from the meeting of the Avonbeg and Avonmore some four miles away. Those who understand the creative processes will not be surprised to learn that Moore himself declared, 'The fact is that I wrote the song in neither place.'

Just before Rathdrum is yet another place that, for many, is hallowed Irish ground – Avondale, once the home of Charles Stewart Parnell. The great patriot (whose obelisk monument stands in O'Connell Street, Dublin) was descended from a Protestant landowning family from Congleton in Cheshire. Born at Avondale on 27 June 1846 when Ireland was in the grip of the Great Famine, Charles Stewart appears to have inherited many anti-English ideas from his mother but later insisted it was stories of the '98 horrors that influenced him most. As a gentleman, of course, he could not envisage himself as a pitchfork-wielding revolutionary and believed Irish salvation lay in constitutional

This massive castle at Kilkenny was built by Strongbow himself. It passed into the hands of the Butlers, one of the great Norman Irish families, in 1391.

politics. At Westminster he conceived the idea of the filibuster, making long-drawn-out speeches about nothing in particular that obstructed the ordinary business of Parliament. His tactics enraged English MPs but forced them to notice Irish grievances. Meanwhile a 'Land War', to which he eventually lent his name, broke out in the Irish countryside: unfair landlords were boycotted or rents were not paid. Parnell neither urged nor condoned violence but property was destroyed and the odd landlord was shot. The campaign proved so successful that an Irish Land Tenure Code was eventually introduced, giving peasants the right to buy the land they rented and Government loans to finance the purchase. The traditional Irish peasant did not disappear overnight but very soon he had become an independent farmer working his own sod, far ahead of most of his European counterparts, including Englishmen. Parnell, meanwhile, had concluded that Home Rule was the only solution for Ireland's problems and began pressing hard for it. Then *The Times* accused him of being implicated in terrorism and in the assassination in Phoenix Park of two British ministers responsible for running the country. When a Special Commission proved the basis of the charges as forgery, Parnell's stature reached its apogee; he became the idol of London society and the 'uncrowned king of Ireland'.

On the very verge of achieving Home Rule for his country in November 1890, his career was ruined when the blackmailing Captain O'Shea — with whose English wife, Katharine, Parnell had been living since 1886 — abruptly exposed him. O'Shea had been a complaisant husband: he was hoping for a financial settlement from his wife when she inherited her aunt's fortune and also for preferment in his career by Parnell. When neither was forthcoming he sued for divorce. The shock to Victorian opinion in both

---

The Long Gallery, Kilkenny Castle. Both Edward VII and George V of England were lavishly entertained here during their visits to Ireland.

England and Ireland was comparable with the sensation created in the 1930s when Edward VIII's affair with Mrs Simpson became known. Gladstone, who had already promised Parnell a Home Rule Bill declared that if Parnell did not step down as Irish leader he would resign the premiership. The Irish Party quickly withdrew their support and Parnell fought on as an ordinary MP amid a campaign of vituperation, calumny and even mob violence. On 26 June 1891 he married Katharine at Steyning in Sussex. But everything had gone wrong and less than four months after his marriage, on 6 October 1891, this proud man, who had had an immense victory abruptly snatched from his grasp, died of pneumonia, his health already broken. He was buried with all honour in the Irish national mausoleum in Glasnevin cemetery, Dublin.

The grounds of Avondale lie mainly on the west bank of the Avonmore. They now constitute a fine forest park of over five hundred acres, with miles of woodland paths and roads where walkers can roam at will amid splendid trees and wildlife. Avondale House itself is a simple Georgian structure dating from 1777; it passed to the Parnells in 1795 but, heavily encumbered by debt, was sold shortly after Charles's death. Only a portion of the house is open to visitors but this includes the unusually high-ceilinged hallway, the sitting room and the beautiful Blue Room which has fine plasterwork and some of the furniture Parnell himself used.

We now retrace our steps to Woodenbridge and then bear right to the village of Shillelagh, famous for its oaks from which oak clubs or shillelaghs were once fashioned. This was an all-purpose instrument, used as a walking stick or cattle prod, for playing hurley, for beating off dogs and for cracking heads. Throughout the eighteenth century, however, the oak woods rapidly disappeared as English owners found it more profitable to sell the wood to London merchants for pipe staves. The shillelagh was of such universal use in Ireland that blackthorn was eventually substituted for oak. It became increasingly famous throughout the world in the same way as the Zulu knobkerrie, but the 'traditional' shillelagh now touted to tourists and

Tynan's Bridge House bar, Kilkenny, finds its reflection in every small town in Ireland.

dressed up in green ribbons is invariably blackthorn and so not a true shillelagh at all.

I suggest you now continue west towards Tullow, which has a picturesque bridge over the Slaney, and take in Browne's Hill dolmen, two miles east of Carlow town, an enormous, single-chambered grave with a truy colossal granite capstone; the largest in Europe, it measures twenty feet square by five feet thick and weighs over a hundred tons. One end rests on two flat slabs, the other on three six-foot-high upright pillar stones. It sits in the middle of a cornfield, looking like a monster from outer space.

One of Ireland's most splendid urban vistas is, without doubt, the sight of Kilkenny Castle, partly Norman, partly nineteenth-century aggrandizement, towering over the placid Nore at the very heart of the ancient city of Kilkenny, one of the few towns in Ireland worth an extended prowl. Since 1391 the castle, built on the site of a Strongbow fortress, has been the ancestral home of the Butlers, ennobled as dukes of Ormonde, who were rivalled only by the Geraldines as the country's greatest Norman family. They were really Fitzwalters but Henry II bestowed on one of them the title 'Chief Butler of Ireland' (for setting duty on wine imports) and they adopted the name. Centuries later a female Butler married an English landowner called Sir William Boleyn, and their joint line produced Anne Boleyn, mother of Queen Elizabeth and the woman who caused Henry VIII's break with Rome. By siding with Henry VIII in this dispute the Butlers gained supremacy over the Kildare Fitzgeralds, and Thomas, the 'Black Earl', was brought up at Windsor as a companion to the future Edward VI. At the Restoration the family got back the Ormonde dukedom it had lost during the Protectorate and Butlers became Viceroys, with estates extending from the Shannon to Waterford city.

At the turn of the twentieth century the Ormondes were still being treated like royalty in Kilkenny, driving in an open carriage drawn by a pair of greys, with people curtseying and bowing as they passed. In April 1899 the future George V and Queen Mary spent a five-night holiday in the castle, where they were entertained in the great 120-foot-long picture gallery, whose crimson walls were hung with portraits by Holbein, Van Dyck, Lely and others. In the spring of 1904 Edward VII and Queen Alexandra, having attended the races at Punchestown and a gargantuan dinner party thrown by Lord Iveagh, head of the Guinness clan, in his Dublin mansion, processed to Kilkenny. New baths, with hot and cold running water, were specially installed for the visit.

Jerpoint Abbey, Co. Kilkenny. Founded in 1180 but largely remodelled in the fifteenth century, it is one of the most impressive of Norman Irish remains.

WEXFORD AND THE INVASION ROUTE

At 5.30 one morning in May 1922 the castle was occupied by Republican Irregulars who informed Lord and Lady Ossory (the Ormondes' son and daughter-in-law) that they had orders to 'defend' it; the Commandant explained that he had no wish 'to be disturbing herself or your Lordship at all'. For two days the Ossorys and their servants dodged bullets while the Irregulars fired machine guns they had set up in the castle towers and the attacking Free State forces replied in kind. Precious furniture and *objets d'art* were smashed and the famous picture gallery, riddled with bullets, became a mess of broken glass and torn pictures. Then at 7 pm on the second day there was a tremendous crash, followed by wild cheering as a Free State armoured car and a party of soldiers broke through the main gate. The Republicans loosed off the rest of their ammunition into the air and surrendered. Crowds of cheering townspeople gathered to congratulate the Ossorys, shaking their hands and showering blessings on them. Even the Irregulars, as they were marched off to prison, insisted on shaking them by the hand and wishing them luck, the Commandant inquiring solicitously, 'I hope herself was not frightened?'

Kilkenny (often called 'the marble city' from the use of a local limestone which has a deep black shine when polished) is a likeable town, despite the fact that it is now so choked with cars that it has had to install traffic lights. Apart from the castle, there are several sites worth seeing: more than a dozen churches or church sites, the Shee almshouses (1584), the Tholsel, or Town Hall (1761) and Rothe House (1594), the home of a rich merchant, which has picturesque courtyards separating its three main blocks. Kyteler's Inn was the home in the fourteenth century of Dame Alice Kyteler who, accused of witchcraft, fled to England and left her maid behind to be burned at the stake in her stead. Medieval and tudor houses are, of course, almost two a penny in

Carrick-on-Suir at dawn. An unpretentious little town, Carrick is tucked under the mountains of neighbouring Co. Waterford.

England but in Ireland they are as rare as rainbows in the Sahara. From St John's bridge, it is possible to glimpse the fine eighteenth-century Kilkenny College building, alma mater of such eminent figures as Swift, Berkeley, Congreve, Farquhar and even Earl Beatty of Battle of Jutland fame.

Two churches stand out: the Black Abbey of 1226 (named for the black robes of its founding Dominican Order), which is still in daily use, and the magnificent St Canice's (Protestant) Cathedral, built on the site of a monastery founded in 577 by St Canice, after whom the city is named. Erected on the site of an earlier romanesque church, the present structure dates basically from the thirteenth century but has been much restored and altered. It suffered during the Reformation when all traces of Catholicism were swept away, and then the Cromwellians really got to work on it; not content with stabling their horses in it, they pulled off the roof, took away its bells, broke all the windows and carried off all the doors as well as defacing and ruining much of what was left. Fortunately, some tombs of the Butlers, including the effigy of a mail-clad Crusader knight, still remain. A round tower, minus its apex, hugs the cathedral walls, and the public can ascend the interior for a fine view of the city.

Kilkenny's history encapsulates much of what went wrong with English–Irish relations over the centuries. In 1361 the Crown, alarmed at the way many Normans were becoming 'more Irish than the Irish themselves', passed the Statutes of Kilkenny which, I suppose, could be described as a kind of apartheid. The idea was to emphasize to the Normans that ultimately they depended on the Crown for their protection and prosperity, a move designed to keep Ireland closely bound to England. The English inhabitants were forbidden to marry the Irish or sell them horses or arms, and had to keep the Irish out of their churches; they had to speak English, use English bows and arrows, ride their horses in the English style (with a saddle) and eschew the game of hurling. From the Irish viewpoint, the really diabolical aspect of the Statutes was that Irishmen were forbidden to obtain redress for any wrongs in Anglo-Norman courts. As their own

Brehon Laws (based on a complex legal and social system handed down from pagan times) could not be applied to the English, this meant that there was no legal barrier to Norman wrongdoing.

In October 1642 a great Catholic Confederacy (or parliament) met in Kilkenny to give legal force to the murderous 1641 Rebellion which had been sweeping Ireland for almost a year, and which had already claimed thousands of lives, many in Ulster; there the native Irish had dealt harshly with Scots settlers, most of whom had come over from Galloway and Lowland Scotland following the Ulster Plantation of 1603. Britain itself, of course, was in turmoil at this time. Scotland had resisted the king's attempt to impose Anglicanism and Charles had, indeed, already raised his standard against Parliament. The Irish outbreak, siding with the king, was a demand for the rectification of Catholic grievances: 'If the Scots may fight for their religion, why should we not do the same?' Fears that the Roundheads intended the total extirpation of the Catholic religion also fanned the flames.

The story of the 1641 Rebellion and subsequent war, which in turn led to the Cromwellian onslaught, is far too convoluted to be more than briefly sketched here. On the Irish side, the fighting was marked by the genius of Owen Roe O'Neill, nephew of the great Earl of Tyrone who, holding high rank in the Spanish army, returned to Ireland to help the Catholic cause. In no time he had welded the Catholics of Ulster into a highly efficient army which, in June 1646, won a brilliant victory at Benburb over a combined English-Scots-Ulster settlers' army, led by the experienced Scots general, Munroe; the Catholics left three thousand Protestant dead – the greatest defeat ever suffered by British arms in Ireland.

At the same time negotiations were under way with the king who desperately needed ten thousand Irish soldiers if he was to turn the tide against Parliament. Charles offered the redress of many Catholic grievances, and in that moment England's history was determined by what happened in Ireland. The decisive factor was the advice of Cardinal Rinuccini, the papal nuncio, who had arrived in Kilkenny with ample funds from Rome and from Cardinal Mazarin, the French Prime Minister. Rinuccini, who was charged with securing the restoration of Catholic primacy in a country overwhelmingly Catholic, advised against the king's terms, and O'Neill, reluctantly, backed him. And so the chance was lost. In England Charles was beheaded and in August 1649 a vengeful Cromwell landed in Ireland with twenty thousand zealous Roundheads. Less than two months later Owen Roe, the only Catholic commander capable of withstanding him, died, and in March 1650 the Confederacy dissolved itself and Kilkenny surrendered.

I suggest you now take the road to Thomastown, to the south-west of which, on the banks of the Little Arrigle river, stands in solitary majesty the great abbey of Jerpoint, possibly the most appealing and rewarding of all Irish Cistercian abbeys. A daughter house of Mellifont, it was acquired by the Ormondes after the Dissolution and held by them until the seventeenth century. Coming upon it in the lonely Irish countryside, with its imposing fifteenth-century tower and surrounding battlements, quite macerates the senses, and closer inspection allows it to speak even more eloquently; the fifteenth-century cloisters have a beauty, tranquillity and spirituality hardly of this world, while the panels on the flat-sided columns, carved with animals and human figures of a superb clarity, seem, as one strolls past, to unfold like a Chaucerian frieze. Inside the church itself there are a number of interesting grave slabs, and the carved stone tomb chests in the chancel, with effigies of Butlers and knights in mail, are outstanding.

We now move through postcard-pretty countryside towards the delightful village of Inistioge (pronounced Inishteeg), with the Nore rippling quietly between well-wooded gorges. The village took me by surprise, with its charming centrepiece of an eighteenth-

Ormonde Castle at Carrick-on-Suir was built by an Earl of Ormonde in anticipation of a visit from Elizabeth I of England: she never arrived.

century ten-arched bridge hung with valerian, and its square, which has a neatness and old-world look about it that would not be out of place in the Cotswolds. Inistioge grew up around an early thirteenth-century Augustinian Friary, portions of which are incorporated in the local Protestant church.

I would recommend now, if time is not too pressing, a slight detour to the small market town of Graiguenamanagh, another pleasant spot on the River Barrow where you will see herons fishing in the bubbling weir. The real attraction here, however, is Duiske Abbey, founded in 1204, the largest Cistercian abbey in Ireland; although altered and added to, it has been lovingly preserved and restored and is in full use today. The thirteenth-century interior, which has not been altered, has a stern ascetic beauty. The exuberant processional doorway, heavily decorated with romanesque carvings, is one of the finest to have escaped Reformation destruction, and outside the north wall of the chancel is a remarkable relic of the sixth century, a baptismal font.

Our route now takes us into Co. Tipperary, aiming for the gracious little town of Carrick-on-Suir. Some five miles before Carrick, however, I suggest you stop briefly at Ahenny, which has two of the oldest and finest high crosses in the country. The carvings have suffered erosion but it is still possible to make them out clearly enough – representations of Daniel in the Lion's Den, processions of monks, animals and some abstract motifs. Both crosses are believed to date from the early eighth century. Carrick has a town square named after its local hero, Sean Kelly (a champion cyclist), and one of the few surviving Elizabethan manor houses in Ireland. It was built by 'Black Tom' Butler so that he could entertain Queen Elizabeth but, possibly as a result of some discreet advice, she never risked setting foot in the sister island. Today the house is in danger of

Ardmore, Co. Waterford. The west wall of the twelfth-century cathedral has remarkable romanesque arcading carved with biblical scenes.

collapse and has been closed to the public. Beside it are the remnants of a much older Butler fortress where, tradition has it, Anne Boleyn was born. This is just possible as one of the later titles of her father, (Sir Thomas Boleyn), was Earl of Wiltshire and Ormonde.

As we make for Clonmel ('the honey meadow') we begin to leave the placid, well-fed face of Ireland, with its fine acres of fertile land, contented cattle and Anglo-Irish ordered beauty, and see signs of a more rugged and spectacular countryside. Away to our right is Slievenamon, 2368 feet high, and to our left the dramatic Comeragh Mountains, which peak at 2600 feet; behind them, to the south, are the Monavullaghs. Clonmel, birthplace of Laurence Sterne, author of *Tristram Shandy*, is now one of the largest inland towns in Ireland. Though it is relatively well-preserved, with old quayside mills fronting the Suir and largely untouched back treets, it is a bustling place, typical perhaps of a new commercially-minded Ireland gorged on EEC funds and anxious to anchor itself firmly as a modern European state. Both George Borrow, who lived here for a while (and took the trouble to learn Irish), and Trollope, who worked in the local post office, would have been astonished to see what was until recently a sleeply old town, blossoming with smart boutiques, delicatessens, cafés and up-market bakeries. Prosperity oozes everywhere: Clonmel is the headquarters of Irish greyhound racing, and it is not uncommon to see men in shops, pubs or hotels carrying great wads of notes in their pockets. It is a good place for fishermen, and in early September you can catch salmon free by simply dipping your line in the Suir from the quayside. Proof of the town's prosperity lies in the large number of excellent hotels and restaurants. At one of Clonmel's oldest hostelries, now very smartly done up with deep-pile carpet and spaciously laid-out tables, I tried a 'Gaelic steak'. Connoisseurs may argue that the best Scottish and English beef is generally superior to Irish but this was fillet steak, smothered in a concoction of Irish whiskey and cream, and it turned out to be one of the best steaks I can ever remember eating.

Historically, Clonmel was the one town in all Ireland

that somehow managed to do what must have seemed the impossible – bamboozle Cromwell. Waterford successfully defied him but Clonmel fooled him. Following Owen Roe O'Neill's death, his nephew Hugh led the remnants of the Ulster army to strengthen southern resistance. Cromwell took a severe drubbing, with some fifteen hundred men dead and many wounded in his efforts to take the town. Finally Hugh O'Neill advised the mayor to treat with the Lord General; Cromwell, perhaps irked by his losses and aware of the effect the Irish climate was having on his men, agreed extremely generous terms for the town's surrender. As soon as this was done O'Neill and his men slipped away in the darkness, thus eluding the net. To his credit, Cromwell stuck to the terms.

As you approach the valley of the Blackwater you will be travelling through some of Ireland's softest and loveliest countryside – lush, rich, a paradise for fishermen – a civilized sort of landscape made picturesque by an amalgam of emerald woods, silver waters and blue mountains. The pass called 'the Vee' cuts a way along the slopes of the fabled Knockmealdown Mountains (2809 feet high), yielding some magnificent vistas. A turn-off will lead you to the celebrated Trappist monastery of Mount Melleray.

The town of Lismore ('The Great Rath') in Co. Waterford is dominated by a fairytale castle that is the Irish residence of the dukes of Devonshire. A famous occupant was Lord Charles Cavendish who married Adele Astaire, Fred Astaire's sister, in 1932 and lived in Lismore Castle until his death. A vast, quasi-regal Victorian edifice perched on a rock overlooking the Blackwater river, it stands on the ruins of a castle built there by Prince John when he was Governor of Ireland from 1199 to 1216. John, naturally, proved himself intensely unpopular in Ireland, his favourite pastime being to pull the beards of Irish chieftains and then encourage his entourage to do the same. In 1589 the castle passed to Raleigh, who hoped to exploit the vast area of tillage, pasture, minerals and fishing rights that went with it, but having, on a visit to England, made one of the queen's maids-of-honour pregnant, he instead found himself locked up in the Tower. In 1602,

in an effort to raise money for his quest for El Dorado, he sold the estate to Richard Boyle, later Earl of Cork, who encouraged many Dorset families to settle here. Boyle's son, Robert was, of course, the father of modern chemistry and author of Boyle's Law. (London also owes a debt to the Lismore Boyles – the fourth earl was the architect of the Royal Academy's headquarters in Piccadilly.) In 1753 the great castle passed by marriage to the dukes of Devonshire, and it was in the early 1800s, during the incumbency of the bachelor sixth duke, that alterations produced the present awesome pile and the beautiful gardens surrounding it. The duke brought over Joseph Paxton, who had just completed the great conservatory at Chatsworth, to assist in the reconstruction. He restored the medieval chapel as a fantastic ballroom while Pugin designed most of the chimneypieces and also the great banqueting hall which looks not unlike a small House of Lords.

Two important discoveries were made here when in 1811 workmen found a crozier and a book in the walls. The crozier, a magnificent bronze and gilt affair, had belonged to Lismore's bishop from 1090 to 1113. The vellum manuscript was a find of inestimable value dating from the fifteenth century and containing many historical tracts. A monastery had been founded here in the early seventh century by St Carthach (or Carthage) – among its later students was Alfred the Great of England – and in the eighth century Lismore had become one of the country's most important ecclesiastical sites, a place of pilgrimage for Irish kings. Sacked six times by the Vikings, it was eventually wiped out completely by Strongbow himself. Today there are two fine churches in what looks like an English town, both bearing the name of St Carthage. The Protestant cathedral, medieval in origin, is largely a seventeenth-century reconstruction with a pretty, even frivolous, spire of 1827 by George Pain, a pupil of Nash. The Catholic church dates from the 1880s.

Waterford City at dusk. On the left is Reginald's Tower, a Norman structure dating from the twelfth century and the oldest building in the city.

We now drive south towards Ardmore, skirting the demesne of Dromana Castle where you might find yourself rubbing your eyes in disbelief as an exotic sight looms in front of you – a gateway raised in the Hindu-Gothic (or Brighton Regency) style, a dazzle of onion domes and minarets that could well herald the entrance to the Taj Mahal at Agra. This was put up in the early nineteenth century by Lord Stuart de Decies, MP and friend of Daniel O'Connell. Interest in India was at its height in Ireland at this time as many Irish officers and ranks were serving there. Dromana, a Fitzgerald stronghold for centuries, came into the Villiers family in the early seventeenth century and they still own it. Perhaps the castle's principal claim to fame, however, is that it was the home of the old Fitzgerald Countess of Desmond: a Methuselah of a woman, she reputedly lived to the age of 162. Raleigh mentions her in his *History of the World* and Bacon cited her as an example of the exceptional longevity of the Irish people. She married during the reign of Edward IV, danced with Henry VII at least a hundred years before she died, and vigorously walked the whole way to her reception at the court of Elizabeth I. Tradition claims she grew three sets of teeth in her adulthood, a new set growing each time she cast off the old. She died when she fell out of a tree while trying to pick cherries and nuts.

Ardmore, magnificently situated overlooking a lovely bay and what is now called the Celtic Sea, is one of those serene Irish beauty spots that do not appear to replicate themselves anywhere else on earth. The Old Parish of Ardmore claims to be the oldest in the country; the original monastic settlement here was founded by St Declan, who had been converted to Christianity in Roman Britain, preceding St Patrick's mission by some thirty years. The locals, it is said, resisted Patrician influences when they finally arrived,

The graceful proportions of this square in Waterford belie the higgledy-piggledy nature of the city's street plan, laid out by the Vikings who founded the city.

based as they were on Roman teachings. As you wander round this delightful site, with its round tower and medieval cathedral, and view the little village and the spreading, deserted sands hazing into blue water below, it is hard to imagine strife or disagreement of any kind afflicting this place. The round tower here is, by common agreement, the finest and most beautiful in all Ireland, marked by a regularity of masonry, a subtly tapering shape and the string courses which encircle it at cunningly unequal intervals. Almost 96 feet high, it is believed to have been the last round tower built in the country. Inside the long, low romanesque cathedral, which dates from the twelfth century, are ogham stones but the unique feature of the building is its west external wall: in thirteen recessed panels resting on top of two much larger ones are exquisite sculptures showing the Fall of Man, the Weighing of Souls, the Judgement of Solomon, the Adoration of the Magi and other biblical episodes.

The road to Dungarvan, the administrative capital of Co. Waterford, can prove to be sheer delight at certain times of the year. In May and June the hedges alongside the roads blaze with thrift, which gathers everywhere like exotic pink hoar frost. A short diversion here will take you to Helvick Head, where you can savour some magnificent Irish coastal scenery – great slashes of folding land striking towards the sea and ending in a succession of abrupt cliffs. Away to the left the foothills of the Monavullaghs, composed like the Comeraghs and Knockmealdown of Old Red Sandstone, also reach out for the sea, gradually giving way, as you travel east, to rocks of volcanic origin.

Dungarvan overlooks its harbour and a wide bay surrounded by heights thick with pine forests. In itself it is not a particularly distinguished town, although it has a fine beach, the first in a succession of strands running east to Waterford Harbour and beyond.

Nearby, at Ballinamona, is a neolithic court cairn (extremely rare in the province of Munster) while in a limestone cave at Kilgreaney two human skeletons were found in 1929 dating from 9000 BC, when Ireland was still physically joined to Britain. The county of Waterford appears to have been the landing point for

the neolithic men who later, moving northwards, erected the great monuments in the Boyne valley.

There are two roads from Dungarvan to Waterford city – the direct route through Kilmacthomas and the slower, if more spectacular, coastal route. Kilmacthomas was the birthplace in 1797 of the actor and comedian Tyrone Power, whose great-grandson and namesake was the Hollywood film star. The coastal route offers wonderful views of Dunbrattin Head, Great Newton Head, the vast spread of Tramore Bay, Brownstown Head and the famous Hook Head. I say 'famous' because the name has become part of a well-known English idiom: inside Waterford Harbour is the village of Crooke, and it was while he was besieging the stubborn defenders of Waterford that Cromwell swore to take it 'by Hook or by Crooke' (in fact he was repulsed, and although he later returned he finally gave up the siege, Waterford holding out for many months more before surrendering to Ireton). There are several pleasant little coves and beaches along this stretch where you can enjoy a dip in the sea. Tramore will put you off if you do not like such places as Blackpool, Brighton or Torremolinos, although its three miles of magnificent beach (the name means 'the great strand') are never overcrowded, even at the height of the season. If you do visit Tramore Bay you may well wonder what the five tall, mysterious-looking stacks are for: they are, in fact, land-based buoys erected in the late eighteenth century to warn sailors of shallow waters. One of these buoys, a painted iron statue of a sailor, is known as the Metal Man, and tradition has it that any girl who hops around the base three times with one foot off the ground will marry within a year.

Waterford city remains one of the most intriguing and interesting of all Irish urban centres – an important crossroads where several of the principal players in

Dunmore East, Co. Waterford. This busy fishing port is popular with anglers and with holidaymakers, who come for the fine sandy beaches.

British and Irish history met. The first Celts to arrive here, the Deisi from Gaul, reached their apogee when they successfully raided and for a while colonized parts of Britain as the Roman Empire gradually collapsed. In 914 Vikings under King Sitric threw walls round a settlement they called Vadrafjord, which quickly became a strong and independent city state, owing allegiance neither to the Irish Church nor to any Gaelic king. It took Strongbow only a day to take the city, however, and he had the Norse king beheaded.

One of the city's main attractions is Reginald's Tower, an old Norse fortress dating from 1003; heavily restored, it still stands at the end of a long succession of quays and has now been made a civic museum housing several royal charters from Tudor times and a unique Charter Roll of 1394. The city remains intensely proud of its associations with British royalty. Three years after Strongbow's arrival Henry II landed with a splendid army intended to overawe both Gaelic and Norman lords and declared Waterford 'a royal city'. It was dazzled again when Richard II landed here in 1394 with easily the greatest, gaudiest and most colourful army ever seen in Ireland – thirty thousand archers, four thousand men-at-arms and a retinue of knights, advisers and prelates. In 1487 loyal Waterford withstood a six-week siege by the Pretender, Lambert Simnel, and in 1495 a twelve-day assault by the second Pretender, Perkin Warbeck, as a result of which a grateful Henry VII bestowed on it the royal motto 'Urbs intacta manet Waterfordia' ('Waterford Unconquered City'). It stuck doggedly to its tradition of loyalty in fiercely opposing Cromwell and in receiving James II in truly regal fashion. Throughout the medieval period Waterford had been second only to Dublin as the centre of Anglo-Norman power and it continued to prosper until the seventeenth century. By the end of the eighteenth century, though its mile-long quays stretching along the Suir were described as Europe's finest, it had become no more than an elegant backwater. The manufacture of glass, begun in the late 1780s, helped to revive its fortunes, however, and Waterford Crystal is now one of Ireland's major exports – extremely beautiful if very expensive –

although by common agreement, modern processes have not *quite* been able to match the exquisite eighteenth-century originals.

Today Waterford is a thriving, bustling, go-ahead place, its long quays choked by that modern curse, the motor car. Behind the waterfront is an industrial park sustaining some thirty-six successful industries. Away from the main streets lie a succession of narrow, ancient byways which are worth exploring. There is, in fact, an excellently signposted 'Historical Trail' which will lead you in easy steps to everything worth seeing. Architecturally, Waterford owes much to John Roberts, a local man and great-grandfather of Field-Marshal Earl Roberts of Kandahar and Waterford (who commanded a brilliant campaign that relieved Mafeking and won the Boer War). In 1770 Roberts built Christ Church (Church of Ireland) Cathedral, considered one of the country's most impressive. It boasts an unusual stepped steeple and its spacious interior is well furnished with monuments. The most imposing, if most gruesome, of these is the monument to James Rice, mayor of Waterford during the Wars of the Roses, which displays his effigy on top of a sarcophagus with worms coiling in and out of his ribs and frogs gnawing at his vitals. Roberts was also responsible for the Catholic cathedral, erected at a time when the penal laws were still in force against Catholics, which speaks well for the broad-mindedness of the local citizens. Sited just off the quays in Barronstrand Street, it has heavy pillars and a grandiose façade, and looks the antithesis of the Protestant cathedral. Roberts was also responsible for the City Hall (which includes the Theatre Royal and another small theatre) along the Mall, a handsome road running south-west from Reginald's Tower with some good Georgian houses. An eighteenth-century Waterford chandelier, a truly magnificent piece, is on display in the Council Chamber of the City Hall; under a copy of it, which still hangs in Philadelphia's Hall of Independence, America's Declaration of Independence was signed. The Chamber of Commerce in O'Connell Street, which runs parallel to the quays, is also by Roberts and has a stunning oval cantilevered staircase. Other places worth visiting are the 'French Church', founded in 1240 by the Grey Friars, which was handed over to the Huguenots when they arrived and occupied until 1819; by then only the tower, nave and chancel of the old friary remained.

Waterford is now an active cultural centre. Birthplace of William Vincent Wallace, composer of the opera *Maritana*, it hosts an annual International Festival of Light Opera, has a fine Music Club and Symphony Club and an excellent Regional Youth Orchestra. The Garter Lane Arts Centre is the largest in provincial Ireland while there are also two flourishing theatre companies.

In 1987 the City Corporation carried out extensive archaeological excavations which revealed much of Viking and Norman Waterford. Sixteen Viking homes were uncovered, along with seventy-five thousand artefacts including a rare amber necklace, scabbards, pottery, clothing, footwear and combs fashioned out of deer antlers.

Leaving Waterford City, you might care to look at the little resorts of Woodstown and Dunmore East, a picture-postcard fishing village with Old Red Sandstone cliffs and fine beaches. Alternatively, take the ferry at Passage East and drive back into the rural delights of Co. Wexford, along winding roads with only light traffic, past fertile fields dotted with black-and-white cattle, blackbirds and magpies hanging in the air and a plenitude of castle ruins sprinkling the landscape – once there were 120 castles in this region. There are two edifices you *must* see here. The first is the tremendous Dunbrody Abbey, perhaps the finest ruin in the country, sitting in mournful majesty near a creek which runs north-eastwards from the Barrow. Built in the twelfth century by monks of St Mary's Abbey, Dublin, and a noted place of sanctuary, it became known as the monastery of St Mary of Refuge.

The magnificent remains of Dunbrody Abbey, Co. Wexford, a thirteenth-century Cistercian foundation. It was a noted place of sanctuary before the Reformation.

The cruciform church is one of the largest in Ireland – 200 feet long by 140 feet wide – with six transept chapels lit by narrow windows. A great heavily built central tower, made more massive and impressive by its low height, broods over this splendid ruin. Only a few miles away lies another magnificent relic, the Cistercian abbey church of Tintern Minor, daughter house of Tintern Major in the Wye Valley, Gwent. Romantically situated amid a grove of tall, fine trees, with the cawing of rooks creating a melancholy chorus, it was founded in about 1200 by William, the Earl Marshal, in thanksgiving for his safe crossing of the Irish Sea in a storm. The first monks came from the parent house, which inspired some of the architectural details here. Much more of this minor house remains than of the original Tintern which, for me anyway, possesses an elegance and style lacking in its Irish counterpart. The unusually massive square tower here seems heavy and overbearing. Nevertheless, it is a notable ruin and has been praised as 'everything an Irish abbey should be'.

As we move nearer the coast now, the distinctive cry is that of the mournful, haunting curlew. This coastline is rich in birdlife; in May every year, some seven million birds descend upon it. You may spot kittiwakes, choughs, herons, oyster-catchers, kingfishers, ravens, puffins, razorbills and many others.

Before you are aware of it you are into a wild and scarcely beautiful spot which bears no sign of its historic importance – an immense low depression of grassland and hillocks, one of which is crowned by the ruins of a thirteenth-century church. Once this was Bannow Island; once, too, a town grew up here, only to be buried after centuries by drifting sands (though this did not prevent it from continuing stubbornly to return two MPs to Parliament). Once, too, on 1 May 1169 to be precise, a small force of Norman knights backed by three hundred archers landed here. Only a short distance from this desolate spot, where the outline of defensive ditches and ramparts can still be seen, lies Baginbun, where Strongbow's personal advance party landed, a year almost to the day later. The Irish annalists recorded the incident thus: 'The fleet of the Flemings came to Erin, they were ninety heroes dressed in mail and the *Gaels set no store by them*.' Not even after a small local Irish force, clad only in linen tunics and armed with spears and swords, had been defeated did the Irish realize what was happening.

The Normans themselves saw things otherwise. A traditional rhyme of theirs has come down to us which summarizes what was to be a long tragedy for Ireland:

At the creek of Baginbun,
Ireland was lost and won.

Baginbun, Co. Wexford, where, as the old rhyme puts it, 'Ireland was lost and won'. The earthworks and ramparts of the first Norman invaders can still be seen.

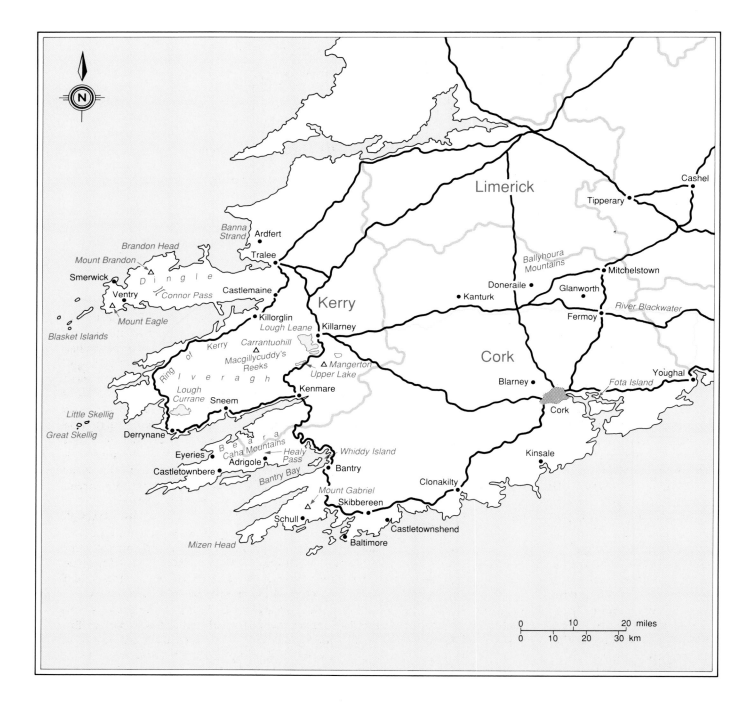

3
Cork and the Great Peninsulas

Cork – Youghal – Cashel – Tralee – The Dingle – Killarney

Ring of Kerry – Beare Peninsula – Mizen Peninsula

Kinsale – Blarney

There is really no need to be frightened of Cork. Merely agree with its poet, Robert Gibbings, who said, 'Cork is the loveliest city in the world. Anybody who does not agree with me either was not born there or is prejudiced'. Corkonians, I should explain, enjoy a terrifying reputation in Ireland; even Dubliners who can (verbally) slit a throat as neatly as anyone on earth, turn wary as cats when they meet a Corkonian, claiming that if he smiles at you it's already too late – the knife's in your back.

The only thing I find palpably wrong with Cork city is its fiendish one-way traffic system. The citizens, despite a baroque fluency which can make them difficult to comprehend, are as warm and helpful as any in Ireland – a notably warm and generous country. I could, of course, be guilty of naivety. When it is a matter of urban landscapes, however, I can be as finicky as a master-chef at a cookery contest, and I have to record that I found nothing in Cork to make me change my mind about Paris or Rome. Nonetheless, it is an agreeable town, beautifully situated on the clear, unbefouled River Lee, at the head of one of Europe's most magnificent harbours.

Cork (from an Irish word meaning 'marsh') was a Viking settlement beside the site of St Finbar's early seventh-century Irish monastery; it was burned by the Irish in 1378 and besieged, bombarded and then burned by John Churchill, later Duke of Marlborough, in the seventeenth century. This means that almost nothing is left of the medieval city, and even its mainly nineteenth- and twentieth-century architecture (with some Georgian relics) suffered serious destruction during the 1920 'Troubles', when the Black-and-Tans (an auxiliary British police force) took hundreds of gallons of petrol from military stores to burn down the centre of the modern city, leaving St Patrick's Street, the principal thoroughfare, a blackened shell.

Thackeray certainly found Cork unlovely, although he was astounded to hear two boys 'almost in rags . . . talking about *one of the Ptolemys*! and talking very well, too. . . Another day', he continues, 'I followed three boys, not half so well dressed as London errand boys; one was telling the other about Captain Ross's voyages, and spoke with as much brightness and intelligence as the best-read gentleman's son in England could do.' (Cork, incidentally, still enjoys a reputation for providing top civil servants, schoolmasters and journalists.) Wesley, on the other hand,

thought it 'one of the pleasantest and most ancient cities in the kindom' – though it seems likely he restricted his perambulations to those spacious avenues which resulted from deliberations of a Wide Street Commission similar to that of Dublin. Macaulay considered University College 'worthy to stand in the High Street in Oxford'; the Court House, with its fine Corinthian portico by G: R. Pain, is most imposing; the dramatic siting of the classically-styled Custom House echoes that of Venice's Dogana; and the famous pepperpot campanile of Shandon's St Anne's (with its great salmon weathervane) would not seem out of place in Tuscany. But Cork never intended itself to be a symbol of architectural splendour; it was devoted to mercantilism, and its old warehouses, stone quaysides and succession of elegant bridges spanning the Lee, which divides round a central island site, show what a busy place it once was. Indeed, many of its streets were navigable waterways, and even today there are capstans in Grand Parade recalling where merchant vessels were moored. It is still a thriving, bustling town – the current population is about 135,000 – engaged in distilling, brewing and bacon-curing, with tanneries, woollen mills, motor works and even a shipyard.

It is a place of strong contrasts, grand establishments sitting side by side with modest little shops or houses, and for the larger part it is free of that modern blight, the chain store. Montenotte, the city's Belgravia, rises in stepped heights reminiscent, say, of Sorrento on a winter's day. Like much of Ireland, which gains from an interplay of cloud and brilliant light, there are dramatic chiaroscuro contrasts in many vistas in the city, especially where the twin channels of the Lee add their own reflective magic to the scene. The view from Patrick's Bridge looks across to the classically pedimented church of St Mary's (a Dominican foundation

---

St Mary's Dominican Church, Cork. The classical façade with its Ionic columns dates from the early nineteenth century.

famed for its miracle-working fourteenth-century image of the Virgin and Child) and beyond to the steep, house-covered hillsides that fade translucently into the background in a numinous image of earth and sky.

North of the river and up an easy incline stands St Anne's. You will notice that two sides of its campanile are made of red sandstone and two of white limestone, but it is the bells – there are eight – one has come to hear (and, indeed, it is possible to arrange to ring them yourself). Their fame comes from a poem written by 'Father Prout', pseudonym of a Cork priest called Father Francis Mahony, who died in Rome in 1866:

On this I ponder
Where'er I wander,
And thus grow fonder,
Sweet Cork of thee;
With thy bells of Shandon,
That sound so grand on
The pleasant waters
Of the river Lee

The modern Church of the Assumption, designed by the noted Cork sculptor Seamus Murphy, is also worth visiting. Pugin's St Peter and Paul is good Gothic Revival. Pain, a pupil of Nash, designed St Patrick's in Lower Glanmire Road, which is the city's finest Catholic church. The lantern spire of Holy Trinity was also designed by Pain but the work was carried out by another architect and is generally deemed none too successful – though worth seeing. Christ Church (Protestant), lying between Grand Parade and South Mall Street, is an eighteenth-century replacement of an earlier church where Spenser is said to have been married, and which was wrecked by Marlborough. St Finbarre's Cathedral (Protestant), whose elegant spires can be glimpsed from all over the city, has a brass marking the grave of the world's first woman Freemason, of whom more anon. The Crawford Art Gallery has an excellent collection of works by Irish artists of the calibre of Orpen, Lavery and Jack B. Yeats.

Cork, city and county both, take due pride in their famous sons, or even adopted sons. Among these are

Michael Collins, a principal architect of the modern Irish state; writers Frank O'Connor and Sean O'Faolain; Father Theobald Mathew (who was actually born in Tipperary but worked in Cork), founder of a hugely successful temperance crusade which saved hundreds of thousands of Irishmen from alcoholic excess; and Daniel Maclise, who painted the House of Lords frescoes. Cork also takes a wry pride in a man called Redmond who in 1766 was hanged for robbery; pronounced dead, he was cut down after nine minutes, but was then restored to health by 'the dint of friction and fumigation'. Redmond, naturally enough, decided to celebrate, and then took it into his head to thank personally the actor, Glover, who had been among those who saved him. That evening he staggered on to the stage where Glover was appearing and caused the audience, who imagined him dead, to lapse into a state of 'terror and consternation'.

Corkonians reserve a certain sardonic pride for the exploits of three of their women. Elizabeth Aldworth bcame the first woman Freemason after she hid herself in a longcase clock in her father's library; since she had witnessed Masonic ceremonies, the Masons were left with no option but to in induct her into the Order. Then there was a Miss Thompson. Seized by corsairs on her way to Cadiz, she was detained in Fez as a slave until rumours of her great beauty reached the Sultan, who removed her to the royal palace. Eventually she was persuaded to become a Moslem and married Muli Mahomed, becoming empress and mother of two of his sons (he had 523 others). The third lady was a real corker. Ann Bonny grew up 'with a fierce and courageous temper'. Her father took her to the West Indies where she married, but she later became acquainted with the notorious pirate, Rackham, who persuaded her to elope with him. Dressed as a man, she sailed alongside him, nobody being 'more forward or courageous than she'. In the end both were caught and sentenced to hang but she was found pregnant and reprieved. She was allowed to see Rackham before his execution but her only words of consolation were, 'If you had fought more like a man, you need not have hanged like a dog.'

Tragedy has never been too far away from Cork city. After the Great Famine a seemingly never-ending river of half-starved emigrants passed through its streets on the way to the dreadful 'coffin ships' that might, or might not, land them in the New World. However, as transatlantic ships grew into great liners and the point of embarkation became Cobh (Cove) in the outer harbour, fewer and fewer passengers were in extremis. Cobh was the Titanic's final port of call, and Cork's dramatic coastline the last land so many of those aboard ever saw.

Further tragedy during the Troubles left Cork numbed. The Tans' main tactic in attempting to defeat insurrection was to terrorize the population . First they assassinated the city's Lord Mayor, then they took to strutting through the streets, slashing at passers-by with riding crops, smashing windows, looting shops and even raping before finally setting fire to the city.

Today Cork has largely forgotten such goings-on and is more concerned with its International Film Festival, and a Montenotte restaurant that is said to be among the best in the British Isles. Yet for all its access to a coastline breeding some of the largest and most succulent shellfish in the world, Cork's great dish is drisheen – a large black pudding variously made with the blood of a sheep, pig, turkey or goose, and stuffed with breadcrumbs, oatmeal, mace and a sprig of tansey, which is reputed to be 'spectacular': not altogether my idea of gourmet eating, all the same.

Before leaving Cork it is worth visiting Fota Island, in the harbour; it has a seventy-acre wildlife park and a famous arboretum, begun in 1820, which contains plants from every continent, with a superb collection from China, Japan and Chile. There is a wonderful Cryptomeria japonica 'Spiralis' – the tallest in Europe – and a spectacular Davidia involucrata, or 'handkerchief tree', from China. The real treasure, however, is

---

St Finbarre's Church of Ireland cathedral, Cork, designed by William Burges in 1867. Its French-gothic spire is a distinctive addition to the city's skyline.

Shop front, Cork. The proprietor has found an imaginative way of attracting customers to otherwise drab premises.

Cork is not only Ireland's largest but possibly its most varied county, the eastern half composed of fertile agricultural land while the west grows ever more rugged and stony, offering immense and beautiful vistas as one surges along straight, seemingly never-ending roads bordered by yellow clumps of waving gorse. Great sweeps of land run down to a coastline whose toothy cliffs, great headlands, coves and indentations are pounded by the wild Atlantic, making it almost the equal of its dramatic rival, Kerry.

Youghal ('Yawl') is of interest because Sir Walter Raleigh's house, Myrtle Grove, still stands in North Main Street although, sadly, it is not open to the public. Raleigh's name lingers ambivalently in the Irish mind. He is credited with introducing the potato, which since his time has been Ireland's staple food (ironically, when he first tasted the berry of the plant he thought it horrible, and it was left to his gardener to discover the role of the tuber); real doubt now exists, however, as to whether he was the first to bring it into the country, the latest evidence being that it was brought from Galicia. As an Elizabethan army captain Raleigh was sent to Ireland to put down the Earl of Desmond's 1579 rebellion, and when the earl's estates were eventually confiscated he was granted forty-two thousand acres. Like his friend Edmund Spenser, with whom he shared many lonely hours discussing poetry, he hated the native Irish. He particularly detested their abuse of whiskey, insisting that they were always drunk, both 'men and women, Gael and Norman alike', and he loathed their method of warfare: 'to fight them is to fight as one beating the air'.

Modern Youghal, situated on the estuary of the Blackwater, is a pleasant enough resort, its best feature, perhaps, being an eighteenth-century clock-tower gate. St Mary's church contains the reputed tomb of the long-lived Countess of Desmond.

Fota House itself, originally an eighteenth-century hunting lodge owned by the family of the earls of Barrymore but redesigned in the 1820s to become one of the best examples of the Irish Regency style. In the 1970s much work was carried out on the interior, with the reintroduction of eighteenth-century furnishings. The collection of eighteenth- and nineteenth-century Irish landscape paintings is the finest outside the National Gallery in Dublin.

A corner turret at Cahir Castle, Co. Tipperary. Set on a rocky islet in the River Suir, the thirteenth-century castle belonged to the earls of Ormonde.

We shall bump into Raleigh again, but I suggest you now head for one of Ireland's most significant sites — the Rock of Cashel in Co. Tipperary. Your route is through Fermoy, Mitchelstown and Cahir, but on the way it is worth taking the main road from Fermoy north-west to Glanworth because on the right-hand side, hidden by trees, stands the truly magnificent gallery grave called Labbacallee (Grave of the Old Woman). It is an astounding sight, 25 feet long, 5 feet wide and 9 feet tall at the apex of its sloping three-slabbed roof. In 1934 a female skeleton was found in the inner chamber and her skull in the outer and larger chamber, where there were also several male skeletons. It dates from 3000 BC and, like others in Munster, appears to have been made by settlers from Brittany. Mitchelstown has a wonderful underground cave system, with stalagmites and stalactites, while Cahir has a picturesque Butler castle sited on a rocky island in the middle of the Suir. This castle was captured in 1599 by Essex, Elizabeth's favourite, one of his few successes in a campaign so disappointing that he fell from favour.

From a distance the Rock of Cashel stands out from the surrounding landscape with the same dramatic force as the spires of Chartres first rise up like a mirage from the waving fields of the plain of Beauce. The 200-foot-tall limestone outcrop dominates sweeping farmlands that end only in the distant blue walls of encircling mountain ranges. The site is among the most haunted in Ireland, a dream-like place clothed in Celtic melancholy. Close up, this Irish acropolis reveals the ruins that crown it: the most exquisite of Irish romanesque churches, 'Cormac's Chapel'; the shell of a grandiose Gothic cathedral; a tower house; a unique early high cross; a 92-foot-high round tower and a fifteenth-century hall of vicars choral.

Cashel was originally the seat of Munster's kings, who claimed to rule the southern half of Ireland and refused to acknowledge Tara's superiority until 859. It was here that Patrick is said to have plucked a shamrock to explain the mystery of the Trinity, and it was also here that he accidentally drove his crozier through the king's foot during baptism; the monarch endured the pain in the belief that this was a symbol of the Crucifixion. In the tenth century a bold Gaelic usurper, determined to put a stop to Norse depredations, seized the kingship from the incumbent MacCarthys and was crowned here in 977. This was Brian Boru, the greatest of all Gaelic kings. In 1101 his descendant handed over Cashel to the Church, and in 1127 Cormack MacCarthy erected his famous chapel on the Rock. Soon a larger edifice was needed and was built alongside it, and it was here that one of the most momentous events in Irish history took place. In 1171 Henry II, backed by a papal bull, called a national synod to round off a century of Church reform. It was this synod, which was also attended by many Irish princes, that recognized Henry as feudal overlord, thus giving legal force to England's right to rule Ireland. A hundred years later this cathedral was replaced by an even larger building, which was set on fire by an Earl of Kildare; when hauled before Henry VII the earl explained that he had merely fired the building because he thought 'the archbishop was in it'. During the Cromwellian wars most of the townsfolk took refuge in the restored building, but were massacred to the last child and the cathedral again fired.

The little gem of a chapel somehow survived all this mayhem, which is the more remarkable when its architectural irrgularities are taken into account: the heavy stone roof is pitched at an apparently impossible angle, the nave arches are off centre, the north tower is more massive than the south and there is a general lack of symmetry in the chapel's construction. Yet the builders managed to orient the structure a few degrees north of east so that the rising sun shines through its altar windows every May, the month of the Virgin to whom it is dedicated.

From Cashel your road now takes you west. Despite the song, Tipperary town itself is not worth stopping

The Rock of Cashel, Co. Tipperary. On top of the limestone outcrop are the ruins of a medieval cathedral, and the most beautiful of Irish romanesque churches.

The eighth-century Gallarus Oratory, Co. Kerry. Built by corbelling and entirely without mortar, it has withstood a thousand years of Atlantic storms.

at, so keep on south-west towards the Ballyhoura Mountains and Doneraile. Four miles north of the town you will find an ivy-clad ruin set in a cornfield, which is all that is left of Kilcolman Castle, Spenser's home, where most of *The Faerie Queene* was written. Spenser, alas, is no more kindly remembered in Ireland than any of the other Elizabethan gentlemen who gained fortunes at the expense of the native population, although the poet himself benefited little. He was sent to Ireland as secretary to the Lord Deputy and was granted an estate following the confiscation of Irish lands. His hatred of the Irish led him at one period to advocate a policy amounting to apartheid and genocide which even the English government found too extreme, and which provoked Viscount Roche to ensure that he was widely ostracized. When insurrection flared again in 1598

Spenser was besieged but managed to escape, leaving his castle to be burned down to the stump it remains today. Back in England, he was coldly received by Elizabeth, to whom he had dedicated his greatest work, and died destitute in 1599.

Aim for Kanturk and then, crossing the border into Kerry, for Tralee, gateway to the Dingle peninsula, one of Ireland's greatest landscapes: desolate yet marvellously beautiful. If you have time you might detour north to Ardfert, where St Brendan's Cathedral has a superb twelfth-century west doorway and the little romanesque church of Tempall na Hoe is worth viewing. A short distance further on is Banna Strand, where Sir Roger Casement landed from a German U-boat on the eve of the 1916 Rebellion and hid out in an old ring fort until discovered; he was subsequently brought to London to be hanged for treason in one of the most sensational trials of the century.

As you start down the thirty-miles-long, mountain-spined peninsula towards Dingle town you will come across Scota's Glen. Here a Scythian called Fenius Farsus, having fled from Egypt (where he appears to have been a military commander) to Spain, first set foot in Ireland, along with his daughter, Scota, and her husband Milesius. Their three names were to live on in the names the Gaelic race has been variously given: the old Irish knew themselves as Feni and later Milesians, while the Romans knew them as Scotti (or Scots); Queen Scota's name lives on in the name Scotland.

Dingle, like all the great peninsulas of the south-west, really demands a volume to itself, and I can offer you only a sketch of it here. There are four major mountainous areas – the Slieve Mish range ('Mountains of Phantoms'), the Stradbally Mountains, Mount Brandon and Mount Eagle – the prevailing rocks being Old Red Sandstone. The coastline, where these sloping hills glide away to end in steep sea cliffs, is interrupted

Dingle Harbour, Co. Kerry, near the foot of the wild and mountainous Dingle peninsula. This small fishing boat is waiting to be repainted.

by occasional inlets and coves. The seemingly immense spaces of the peninsula's three major valleys are broken here and there by lonely cottages, not only emphasizing the remoteness of the area but also enhancing the bulk of the great mountain masses. Everywhere the fields are small, with colour variously springing from ferns, black mosses, fuchsia hedges, wild iris and even orchids. There is much rare flora and fauna quite unknown in Britain. Part of the peninsula is a Gaeltacht, where time seems to stretch to infinity and life is conducted at a wonderfully gentle pace.

This whole finger of land, with its great rock faces and deep gorges, is littered with an almost uncountable number of prehistoric megaliths, souterrains, boundary and ogham stones and early Christian ruins called clochans (or beehive huts) – stone shelters barely four feet high whose occupants, ascetic monks, had to crouch to get into them. Over four hundred clochans alone cling to the slopes of Mount Eagle, between Ventry and Slea Head. From the headland itself there are stupendous views of the other three peninsulas to the south, as well as the Skellig islands, Little Skellig and Skellig Michael. Due west from Dingle are the Blaskets, which were populated until the 1950s and bred some marvellous writers in the Gaelic tongue (the broken, needle-like rocks of Blasket Sound, incidentally, claimed two Armada ships, one of which, the *Santa Maria della Rosa*, has been recovered).

On the north coast of the peninsula lies Smerwick Harbour, a spacious natural inlet whose name still carries a chilling ring for those acquainted with Irish history. At a spot badly misnamed Dun an Oir (Fort of Gold) a horrendous massacre took place in 1580. Beautifully situated on the edge of steep cliffs overlooking a glorious cove, the place gained its name when one of Frobisher's ships carrying what he believed to be gold (in fact, it was pyrites or 'fool's gold') was

The Upper Lake, Killarney, Co. Kerry. Dominated by Macgillycuddy's Reeks and surrounded by virgin forest, it is the second largest of the lakes.

wrecked here. In late September six ships carrying some eight hundred Spaniards, Italians and Irish landed at Smerwick and set about fortifying Dun an Oir. Soon an English fleet arrived and opened a bombardment, while the Lord Deputy, with strong forces, encircled the fort by land. Within three days the Italian commander surrendered, after first giving up two Irish civilians (one a priest) and an English Catholic, all of whom refused to acknowledge Elizabeth as head of the English Church and were tortured and mutilated before being hanged. The officers of the expedition were spared, but more than six hundred ordinary soldiers, along with two Irishmen and all the women who had accompanied the party, were taken into the next field, known as the Field of the Cutting; there they were all decapitated, their heads buried in the field and their bodies tossed into the sea hundreds of feet below. Among the most active executioners that day was Raleigh. Such acts of savagery were not, of course, considered abnormal in those days.

Some five miles from his lovely yet gruesome place, in an area almost too richly endowed with antiquities (twenty-one churches, fifteen oratories, twelve standing crosses, nine so-called 'penitential stations' and seventy-six holy wells) stands the fascinating Gallarus Oratory. Dating from the eighth century, it consists of unmortared stones piled on each other in the method known as corbelling, and it has managed not only to defy twelve hundred years of Atlantic weather but also to keep its interior bone dry. The building is a rectangle, some 15 feet long, 10 feet wide and 16 feet tall, and, although its roof has sagged slightly, it remains the finest example of its kind in the country and unique in the British Isles.

Splendid Mount Brandon (at 3127 feet, Ireland's second highest peak) is named after Brendan (or Brandon), perhaps the most daring of all those extraordinary Irish *peregrini* who travelled as pilgrims wherever fancy took them during the Dark Ages. Born in 484, Brendan and his companions sailed the Atlantic in a currach not unlike those still being built in Dingle, and is believed to have reached America. His story, pieced together by monks years later, became a

The cloister at Muckross Abbey, Killarney. The abbey was built by a MacCarthy chieftain in the fifteenth century for the Franciscans.

medieval bestseller, though it still provides a puzzle for historians (the Portuguese, the greatest sailors of their day, had 'St Brendan's Isle' marked on their maps up till the eighteenth century). Brendan describes places that correspond to Iceland, Greenland, the Azores, the Bahamas and, in particular, parts of America's eastern littoral. The British explorer Tim Severin, travelling in a replica of Brendan's currach, has proved that such a vessel could have reached the New World, and no alternative explanation of the geographical knowledge contained in Brendan's accounts has yet been offered. Suggestions that certain details might have come from later Viking explorers scarcely stand up: there is no evidence that anybody in Ireland had ever heard of the Norse navigator Leif Erikson (whose Vinland claim is doubtful enough) until

modern times, and the belief that Brendan was the first European to reach America cannot be dismissed.

It is still possible to climb a rock-strewn and very steep track up Mount Brandon to the remains of the saint's oratory. Until the eighteenth century this site was the object of Ireland's third most important pilgrimage; today it provides marvellous views over rugged mountain scenery to the Atlantic and the superb peninsular coastline. Do not miss making a trip over the Conor Pass (1500 feet), where the road is flanked at first by immense cliffs on one side and dizzying drops on the other, and then crosses a stony wasteland scattered with giant boulders and interspersed with mountain lakes, great ragged peaks rising all around to awesome heights.

By skirting the south edge of the Dingle to Castlemaine, with the Slieve Mish Mountains on your left, you can rapidly reach the Lakes of Killarney. So many descriptions of this region had been written by as early as 1776 that the traveller Arthur Young complained that he did not intend to add to them (though he did). A warning, however: the Lakes may, at first glance, be a let-down. It is true, of course, that the hype has been such that if they had actually dropped from heaven they could not live up to expectations. The mountains surrounding the Upper, Middle, and Lower lakes (the lower properly called Lough Leane), though romantically hewn, scarcely inspire awe: Mangerton is only 2756 feet, Tomies 2413 feet, Purple Mountain 1739 feet and Torc, down which tumbles the famed Torc Cascade, a mere 1764 feet. Carrantuohill, at 3414 feet Ireland's highest peak, manages to remain largely hidden from view among the other summits of Macgillycuddy's Reeks, and fails to make the same sort of impact as Snowdon or Ben Nevis. But, while the much-touted 'Ladies' View' on the Kenmare road seems to me to reveal little more than the humdrum,

Derrynane Bay, Co. Kerry, where Daniel O'Connell, 'the Liberator', was born. In this remote region, the O'Connells retained their wealth by smuggling.

from vantage points on Lough Leane, with its thirty superb islands, Killarney's amalgam of mountain, stream, lake, exotic vegetation and venerable ruins begins to cast its spell. Arbutuses (or strawberry trees) flourish here, along with saxifrages and greater butterworts that are unknown in Britain; bamboo, eucalyptus, magnolia and other sub-tropical plants thrive in the soft, humid air; rhododendrons have grown so mightily that they have now become a menace: gradually you begin to appreciate that what makes Killarney different from other European lake districts is its sheer lushness. There is much more, of course: cormorants perching on rocks or islets, waiting to pounce; snipe and woodcock rising in sudden flurries into the air; jets of swans or wild geese flapping across the sky; red deer scampering among the densely wooded heights; little black-backed trout darting hither and thither in the waters; and, above all, a special kind of silence.

Queen Victoria thought it all looked 'just like Scotland' which pleased her immensely, although (incredibly!) she disliked 'the heat'. Tennyson found a poem here and Benjamin Britten, who once had a Killarney cottage, found inspiration for a serenade in the poet's words. Even Bernard Shaw, for all his rationalist rigour, was compelled to think the Lakes 'the most beautiful spot on earth'.

To see the region properly, however, you should take to your feet and tramp the shores or climb into the hills: on Mangerton there is a splendid tarn called the Devil's Punchbowl; from the summit of the Paps of Danae (Queen of the de Danaans) you can get a full 360° view of all Kerry; everywhere on these summits you will run across strange, natural wonders. Visit serene Muckross Abbey (in what was once the estate of the Earls of Kenmare), a perfect place to sit and just meditate; look in at nineteenth-century Muckross

---

Macgillycuddy's Reeks in winter, seen from Ballybearna Gap. Peaking at 3314 ft, they are Ireland's highest mountains.

House, from whose windows there are superb views; then proceed along well-worn paths to the Middle Lake, where you can enjoy the enchanting Meeting of Waters and a close-up view of the Torc Cascade. Finally, cap your visit by driving to the Gap of Dunloe, a magnificently sombre, rock-strewn gorge, with jagged, almost perpendicular hillsides, which can be explored on foot or horseback (there are ponies for hire) before descending to the Upper Lake; there you can embark on a boat through the Lakes.

The town of Killarney, though Pugin's St Mary's Cathedral is possibly Ireland's best example of Gothic Revival, should be avoided. Though there is plenty of chat and, of course, live music, it is a maelstrom of package tourism – car-choked streets, jaunting-cars for hire, souvenir shops, guides official and non-official, and nothing of distinction whatsoever.

Thirty years ago the wildness of the 110-mile Ring of Kerry (the Iveragh Peninsula) would have offered the tourist a superb treat but by 1991 it seemed to me to have become just another stop on the package-tourist trail. Waterville, a simple fishing village until the 1960s, was displaying its aspirations to become an Irish Great Yarmouth with holiday crowds and modern amenities, and the once immaculate silences and dark glories of lovely Lough Currane were being besmirched (to my mind) by a Club Mediterranean complex.

Yet much of the old Ireland can still be discerned under the ugly new veneer; dark blue mountains; glinting, silver inland waters; a rugged coastline which offers close-up views of the Skelligs, those spindles of slab and grit with sheer 700-foot drops, where once monks crouched in precariously perched clochans. Your circuit of the Ring begins at Killorglin which, apart from its noted Puck Fair, has little to commend it. The Fair itself is as bacchanalian kind of outburst lasting three days, which sees King Puck, a he-goat decorated with ribbons and rosettes, hoisted onto a platform high above the crowds while a great cattle, sheep and horse fair takes place below. Shops and bars never close and there is wild, if good-natured, dancing, singing and music. The fair's origins are obscure: some say goats warned the townsfolk of Cromwell's

coming but others that it stems from pagan times and descends from the great Celtic Festival of Lughnasa, which celebrated the harvest.

If Waterville disappoints you as it does me, continue south to Derrynane ('Derrynaan'), a wild and rock-bound bay with marvellous beaches. Nearby is Derrynane House, ancestral home of Daniel O'Connell, the great nineteenth-century leader of the fight for Catholic emancipation (whose grandparents, incidentally, made their fortune by smuggling, using these beaches to excellent effect). Further north-east, Rossbeigh Strand, backed by dunes, offers a great sheet of yellow-white sand superb for bathing, walking and gulping in the scenery.

Like Dingle, the peninsula is rich in antiquities, the two most prominent being Staigue Fort and Leacanbuaile. Both are circular, dry-stone structures dating from the Iron Age. Staigue is approached by a narrow road with hedges flowering with hawthorn, bog iris, willow and fuchsia, and stands out massively against a backdrop of boulder-strewn mountain. Its walls are 10–18 feet high and 13 feet thick at their base. The diameter of the fort is 90 feet.

The wilder reaches of the Ring still recall J. M. Synge's words: 'One wonders in this place why anyone is left in Dublin, London or Paris where it would be better, one would think, to live in a tent or hut with this magnificent sea and sky and to breathe this wonderful air which is like wine in one's teeth'. Eight miles north of Sneem, to the east of Staigue Fort, is the Ballaghbeama Gap, a dizzying slash in the mountains, where a narrow road flanked by a tumbling stream twists between cliffs two thousand feet or more high, with the folds of Macgillycuddy's Reeks rising in the middle distance.

Kenmare, which marks the end of the Ring of Kerry, was founded by Sir William Petty, Cromwell's

Bantry House, Co. Cork, dates from 1765. The gardens, laid out in the Italian manner, are superbly sited overlooking the Beara Peninsula.

Surveyor General (who made the first ever survey of Ireland), and planned by his successor, the Marquess of Lansdowne. It was generously laid out and, until twenty years ago, remained a splendid oasis of trim, well-preserved small hotels and guesthouses whose front gardens bloomed with Mediterranean-type trees and shrubs. It also boasted a magnificent wide, airy main street which today alas, is little better than a monster car-park colonized by tourists and cluttered with boutiques and delicatessens. (Sir William Petty, incidentally, had a unique solution to what was, even in his day, the vexed 'Irish problem'. This was to mix the English and Irish populations together, and to this end he suggested the importation of twenty thousand English maidens to Ireland and the export of a similar number of Irish maidens to England.)

The Beara Peninsula, which lies between the Kenmare estuary and Bantry Bay, is, I am told, the least popular of all the great peninsulas of the south-west — which may be why I like it the most; to me it seems nearer to the wilder, lonelier, untouched world that was once traditional Ireland. Physically, it presents a dazzle of extraordinary, patterned Old Red Sandstone formations, signs of ancient and terrible rock upheaval. The road along the northern side of the peninsula, which crosses the county boundary from Kerry into Cork, follows a dizzying zigzag route with startling cliff drops only inches away and superb views of the Iveragh Mountains and the estuary. At Eyeries it is worth seeking out a famous ogham stone which, at $17\frac{1}{2}$ feet high, is the tallest in existence. Return along the southern shore of the Beara, with the wide sweep of Bantry Bay and its numerous islands to your right; to your left are the dark blue mountains of the Caha range which peak at Hungry Hill (2251 feet). Two miles west of Castletownbere stand the ruins of Dunboy Castle; an O'Sullivan stronghold, this was the last Irish fortress to fall to the English following the Gaelic disaster at Kinsale in 1601. At Adrigole you should take the Healy Pass (named for Tim Healy, first Governor General of the Irish Free State), from which you can enjoy magnificent views.

Thackeray wrote of Bantry Bay, 'Were such a bay

lying upon an English shore, it would be the world's wonder'. Running out thirty miles or more before it merges with the Atlantic, it presents as beautiful a scenic drama as any in Ireland. The eye is caught by a backdrop of great mountains and billowing oceans of cloud swinging in from the south, changing the landscape's colours rapidly from stark green to slate grey and then deep azure. The town of Bantry itself squats round a spacious square with a statue of St Brendan boldly challenging the elements sweeping up the bay. It is hard at times to forgive an Irish Government that permitted Whiddy Island to be used for the unloading and storage of American crude oil in terminal tanks whose very presence destroys much of the value of this place. One tries to shrug off such philistinism and concentrate instead on Bantry House, a fine Georgian pile of 1765 which should not be missed. Magnificently positioned facing Beara, with Italian-style gardens, it is simply stuffed with art treasures, many from the French Napoleonic period – paintings, tapestries, carpets, fireplaces – and even *objets d'art* from Versailles, which were acquired in the nineteenth century by the second Lord Bantry.

The landscape of the Mizen peninsula shares much of the character of its fellows – wild, rugged scenery, improbable rock and scrubland, magnificent cliffs, great sandy beaches and stupendous views; the panorama from the summit of Mount Gabriel (1312 feet) is breathtaking. Mizen Head, its westernmost point, itself provides a spectacular, teeth-clenching view, with vertiginous cliff falls of 765 feet. Once one of the poorest and least populated areas in Ireland, Mizen was 'discovered' by hippies in the Sixties, and nowadays the beautiful beaches at Schull and Barleycove attract many visitors. Roaringwater Bay has a magnificent scattering of islands, one of them Clear Island, the home of thousands of sea birds. Since a Bird Observatory was set up here a few years ago many rare species have been observed, including great and little shearwaters and the black-browed albatross.

You are now on your way back to Cork city by way of Skibbereen and Clonakilty, but you may wish to make a slight detour to the other side of Roaringwater Bay, where the attraction is the little fishing village of Baltimore (from which the Maryland city got its name); this is the site of the famous Sack in 1631 when Algerian corsairs descended one night, massacred most of the men and carried off the attractive women to slavery in North Africa.

The coast road now continues to Skibbereen, from which once emanated some of the most harrowing and pitiful descriptions of the Great Famine. Here, too, the local newspaper, *The Skibbereen Eagle*, made its mark on journalistic history by solemnly warning the Tsar: 'We have our eye on you!' The countryside is still beautiful if less dramatic – hedges glowing with gorse and a profusion of wild flowers, with the glint of the sea and the spectacle of great headlands never far away. Small detours will take you to such pleasant oases as Castletownshend, home of Edith Somerville of the famous partnership of Somerville and Ross that produced *Tales of an Irish RM*; to Woodfield, birthplace of Michael Collins; or, fourteen miles north of Clonakilty, to the roadside spot called Beal-na-mBlath where Collins was killed in an ambush by Irregulars in 1922. Also to be seen is the shell of Derry House (burnt out during The Troubles), where Bernard Shaw worked on *Captain Brassbound's Conversion*. Your next stop is Kinsale.

When I first glimpsed this historic harbour I thought the town one of the prettiest in Ireland, encircled as it is with gentle heights, its streets generously laid out with fine, bow-windowed Georgian dwelling-houses and its main square surrounded by picturesque tile-hung properties. The whole scene seemed to me to be reminiscent of England's picture-postcard West Country. It still stands out as almost elegant by Irish standards but, as the haunt of well-heeled anglers and yachtsmen, it has been so self-consciously prettified in recent years that it now looks

Mizen Head, Co. Cork, pokes a lonely, slender finger of land into the Atlantic. The area is rich in beaches, sea-cliffs and archaeological remains.

more like a cheap film set than anything else. What in England is the product of long evolution has here been too smartly replicated with signs, awnings, shop fronts and twee restaurants, in an attempt to produce quaintness that has somehow backfired. Nevertheless, it is a good town for delicious seafood.

Kinsale, of course, reeks with history, little or none of it agreeable to the memory of Catholic and Gaelic Ireland. The Battle of Kinsale, in a sense the Culloden of Ireland, was the most serious attempt since the Norman Conquest to overthrow English power in Ireland. The native Irish were determined to put a stop to the confiscation of Irish land and its settlement by English colonists, and to restore 'Christ's Catholic religion' instead of Elizabeth's Protestant formulations. It ended in disaster on Christmas Eve, 1601.

Following the Desmond rebellion, Elizabeth's solution to Irish problems was to extend royal government to the entire country and strip of his lands any chieftain who refused to bow the knee. In 1595 Hugh O'Neill, a descendant of Ireland's ancient high kings who had been elevated to the earldom of Tyrone, took the decision to join a rebellion which had already been in progress since 1593. This had been instigated by the dashing young Red Hugh O'Donnell, who had convinced many important Ulster chieftains both that they must stand and fight and that they must negotiate with Spain for assistance. O'Neill was a man of exceptional talents and ability; raised at Elizabeth's court, he had been convinced that diplomacy was the best course but now he realized that her policy would brook no compromises. Once he took the field English forces were routed in one engagement after another across the provinces of Ulster and Connacht. In 1598 he inflicted the most dramatic defeat the Crown had yet suffered in Ireland at the Battle of the Yellow Ford, near Armagh; 'since the time the English first set foot in Ireland they never received a greater overthrow', declared the historian Camden. Elizabeth's answer was to appoint two new commanders, Mountjoy and Carew, whose strategy was to lay waste the country, burning, killing and starving out the population and building a series of forts at intervals to pin down O'Neill within Ulster. Finally, in September 1601, the long-promised Spanish help arrived, but it brought only disaster.

The Spanish mistake was to land at Kinsale instead of either on the west coast of Ireland or in Ulster itself. Worse, the Spanish force was negligible and its commander inexperienced; yet O'Neill knew he had to move out and march the whole length of Ireland to join them. He and Red Hugh O'Donnell managed to outwit the covering English forces and reached Kinsale at the end of September, to find Carew and his army sandwiched between themselves and the Spanish. O'Neill appeared to hold all the cards; he had merely to wait and the trapped English army would begin to disintegrate through sickness and desertion. However, the Spaniards pressed for action, and Red Hugh, an impetuous though skilful commander who had been victorious in all previous encounters with English forces, held the same view. Finally O'Neill gave way and agreed to attack in concert with the Spaniards. In the event the Spaniards stayed put and the Irish forces, attacking across open ground, were routed. It was the last gasp of Gaelic Ireland and the beginning of what the native population regards as three centuries of oppression. O'Donnell fled to Spain (where he was poisoned by an agent of Walsingham) while O'Neill carried on fitful rebellion for another two years; realizing the hoplessness of his position, he eventually made formal submission to the Crown. Harassed on all sides, however, by the new men at the court of James I and stripped of his princely powers, O'Neill, along with ninety-nine other leading men of Ulster, fled Ireland in 1607. Their lands were at once seized and given to English and Scottish settlers in what was called the Plantation of Ulster, the principal origin of the problems now agitating Northern Ireland.

Kinsale, Co. Cork. Near by the fate of Gaelic Ireland was decided in 1601, when Spanish help failed to turn the battle in Ireland's favour.

Blarney, just north of Cork, must be the only place on earth whose worldwide fame rests on a single stone; according to legend, to kiss it is to acquire the gift of eloquence. This stone, a limestone block 4 feet long by 1 foot wide, is embedded 83 feet from the ground among the machicolations of Blarney Castle, a fifteenth-century tower and keep beautifully set amid ancient oaks and yew trees in a small village on the outskirts of Cork city. It requires a steady nerve to kiss it as you have to lean out and lower your head some distance, hands gripping iron stanchions and legs held firmly (you hope) by two men as you hang upside down. Ireland is a land replete with myths, legends, stories, fairies, 'little people', ghosts, miracles and vanishing lakes (even one that actually dries out when it rains), but the legend attached to the Blarney Stone is one of its most popular. The story is that Elizabeth I made repeated demands for Cormac MacCarthy, Lord of Blarney, to surrender his castle as part of an armistice. One night, unable to sleep, as he desperately sought to fabricate plausible reasons for resisting, he went wandering in the woods; there he met the queen of the fairies who told him, 'Don't vex yourself. Go home to bed and sleep and in the morning get up at dawn and go outside; there, right before you, you'll see a big stone. Kiss it and you'll never again want for words.' Cormac did so and found words simply pouring from his mouth; indeed he became so eloquent that it was said he could 'talk a noose off his neck'. Afraid that someone else might discover the stone's amazing properties, he had it hauled to the top of his battlements and embedded there in a position almost impossible for anyone to reach. Meantime, Elizabeth continued to press him to conform with her orders, but with 'fair words and soft speech' Cormac would make one promise after another and keep none of them. In exasperation Elizabeth declared, 'This is all blarney; what he says, he never means.' Thus a new word entered the English language. For nearly two hundred years people have been kissing this block of limestone, at great inconvenience and even risk to their lives, hoping for the gift of eloquence.

Blarney Castle, Co. Cork. Once a MacCarthy stronghold, it is the home of the famous Blarney Stone, said to bestow eloquence on anyone who kisses it.

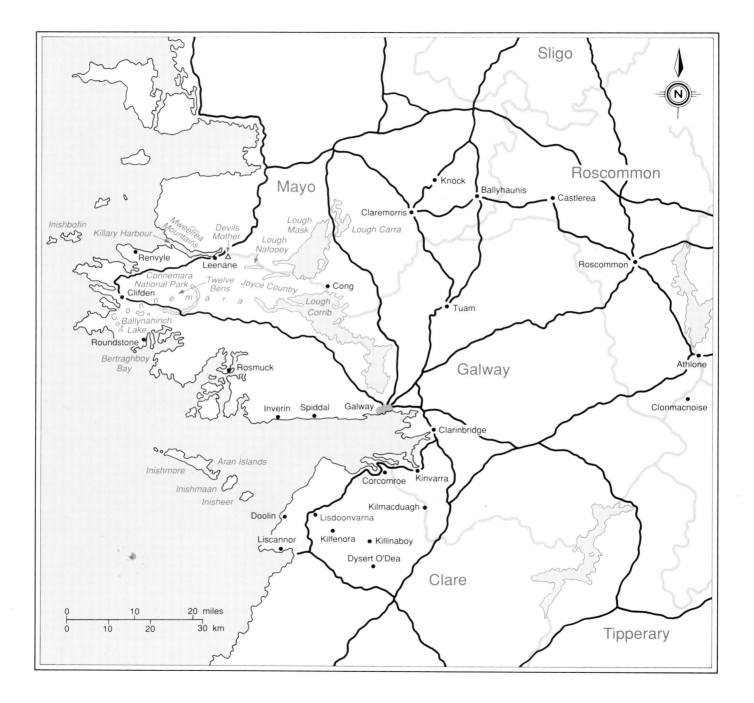

Sligo

Mayo

Roscommon

Galway

Clare

Tipperary

N

Inishbofin

Killary Harbour

Mweelrea Mountains

Renvyle

Leenane

Devils Mother

Lough Mask

Lough Nafooey

Lough Carra

Knock

Ballyhaunis

Castlerea

Claremorris

Connemara National Park

Twelve Bens

Joyce Country

Clifden

C o n n e m a r a

Cong

Lough Corrib

Tuam

Roscommon

Ballynahinch Lake

Roundstone

Bertraghboy Bay

Rosmuck

Galway

Inverin

Spiddal

Galway

Athlone

Clonmacnoise

Clarinbridge

Aran Islands

Inishmore

Corcomroe

Kinvarra

Inishmaan

Inisheer

Kilmacduagh

Doolin

Lisdoonvarna

Liscannor

Kilfenora

Killinaboy

Dysert O'Dea

0   10   20 miles

0   10   20   30 km

4
Galway, the Burren and Connemara

Galway City – The Burren – Cliffs of Moher – Lisdoonvarna
Killinaboy – Kilmacduagh – Coole Park – Clonmacnoise
Castlerea – Joyce Country – Renvyle – Inishbofin – Clifden
The Aran Islands

It is not easy to resist the emollients of a city which erects in its main square a statue to a poet – and a little leprechaun of a fellow at that, of whom almost nobody has ever heard. Padraic O'Conaire once wandered around Connemara telling stories and writing tales and poems in Irish; in the pre-television age he was the walking relic of a millennia-old Irish tradition. Galway, with its long cosmopolitan history, delightfully flaunts its civilized values by celebrating a poet whose fame, such as it is, will never add a pfennig to its tourist budget.

The city, named for a Celtic king's daughter who drowned in nearby Lough Corrib, is exhilaratingly situated in one of the wildest parts of Ireland, at the head of a magnificent bay directly facing the open Atlantic. Originally a collection of huts, it was seized in the thirteenth century by the Normans who colonized it with fourteen families, later to be contemptuously dubbed by the Cromwellians 'The Fourteen Tribes of Galway'. Their names were Athy, Blake, Bodkin, Browne, D'Arcy, Deane, ffont, ffrench, Joyce, Kirwan, Lynch, Martin, Morris and Skerret, and their armorial bearings still decorate some Galway houses. They soon built it into an important trading port, though they had to contend with repeated attacks from Gaelic clans: an unambiguous inscription over the West Gate reads; 'From the fury of the O'Flaherties, the Good Lord deliver us'.

However, the native Irish were not entirely unjustified. Under the Treaty of Windsor Henry II had agreed that all the country west of the Shannon should remain undisturbed in native hands, but no sooner had he returned to France than Norman barons poured across the river and seized whatever choice acres were going – a pattern of cynical betrayal that was to be repeated many times in Irish history.

The fourteen tribes worked up such a prosperous trade with France and Spain that Galway soon became one of the most successful ports in the British Isles. They jealously protected their interests, even down to practising a form of apartheid: in 1518 they passed a law declaring that 'neither "O" nor "Mac" shalle strutte ne swaggere thro the streets of Galway'. However, in the seventeenth century they twice backed the wrong horse: first, they resisted the Cromwellians and had their town burned down around their ears; second, as loyal Catholics, they backed James II against the Williamites, and as a consequence their commerce

began to languish. It has been slowly helped to recover only quite recently.

Today, Galway's light industries are prospering and a thriving export trade in the beautiful locally-hewn Connemara marble has been established. With some thirty thousand residents, it has become what by Irish standards is a trendy city, a hustling, bustling if still good-natured little place that attracts thousands of young people from all over Europe in the summer season. They come for the whiskey and stout, for the traditional folk music that emanates from dozens of pubs and, in particular, for that form of Irish social intercourse known as 'the crack' – 'Ah, the crack was great!' (meaning everyone had a good time). With a reservoir of educated and enthusiastic young people attending University College (itself based on Oxbridge models) there is a strong impetus towards cultural activity of all kinds.

Apart from the venues for traditional music, there is a plethora of places devoted to jazz and disco dancing. Further up the cultural scale there is the Druid Theatre Company, which stages six new plays, most of them Irish, every year. The Taibhdhearc is an even more famous theatre but demands a knowledge of Irish for it stages plays in that language only. There is also a fine Arts Centre which puts on poetry, music and theatrical performances. The summer scene is marked by a succession of arts, busking and folk music festivals as well as two visually pleasing and rather more ancient celebrations. One is the spectacular blessing of the Claddagh fishing fleet, when all the herring ships, gaily bedecked with colours and rosettes, sail out into Galway Bay; the other is a race across the bay by the traditional turf-carrying Galway Hookers – little ships whose design and origins stem from prototypes still plying the North African littoral.

Nothing, however, could possibly compare with the

Padraic O'Conaire, whose statue occupies pride of place in Eyre Square, Galway, was a poet and storyteller who travelled the roads of Connemara.

The Claddagh, Galway, was once a picturesque, if insanitary, collection of fishermen's cabins. The inhabitants claimed to be the city's earliest settlers.

full-blown excitement and high festivity of the Galway Races, when the town seeks to accommodate at least three times as many people as it has room for. Anybody who manages a night's rest in a bathtub or on a snooker table is said to consider himself blessed. The whole week is a mixture of Cheltenham Gold Cup, the Seville Feria and Derby Day rolled into one, with fun fairs, sideshows and the magnetic attractions of the racecourse's famous long bar (at 210 feet, said to be the longest in the British Isles).

Normally, though, the bustle centres on Eyre Square, dominated at one end by the comforting Victorian solidity of the Great Southern Hotel and at the other by an unexpected modern sculpture consisting of arcs of rusted metal and spouting white fountains symbolizing the sails of Galway Hookers.

123

A detail from Lynch's Castle, Galway, probably the finest medieval town house in Ireland. The Lynches were one of the original 'Fourteen Tribes of Galway'.

Here, during the high season, impromptu musical or theatrical performances might start up at any time of the day or night.

Galway warrants a substantial browse. Lynch's Castle (now a bank) in Shop Street is probably the finest medieval town house in Ireland; for three hundred years the Lynch family were the most prominent in Galway, and it is claimed that they gave their name to lynch law: in 1493, finding no one willing to execute his son who had been found guilty of murder, Mayor Lynch did the job himself. There is a memorial to the event beside the churchyard of St Nicholas's (Protestant) Church, the largest medieval church in Ireland, where Columbus, on a visit to Galway, once prayed. The Catholic cathedral, on the west bank of the River Corrib, is a glaring white limestone construction with an enormous copper dome which has been likened to the back of a giant toad. It is notable only because it is a delirious muddle of architectural styles and a warning against planning by committee. It was erected between 1959 and 1965 through the enthusiasm of the local bishop, Dr Mícheal Browne, and in sconsequence has been cynically dubbed 'The Taj Mícheal' (Mee-hal). Near to this monstrosity, however, is one of Galway's genuine attractions – the Salmon Weir Bridge. Galway is noted for its salmon (and oysters) and it is easy to spend a hypnotic hour or two on this bridge watching the salmon during the spring run; they lie in shoals in the crystal-clear water before making their way up to the spawning grounds in Lough Corrib.

Down by the harbour is a sixteenth-century structure called Spanish Arch, a fragment of the old town walls where ships used to unload wine and rum. For Joycean scholars, a gift shop in Bowling Lane, just off Market Street, is of interest, for this was the home of Nora Barnacle, the novelist's wife.

Unexpected names thrust their way on to the Galway scene. Wilfred Scawen Blunt turned up here in the 1880s, gallantly to aid and exhort the starving peasants of Co. Galway who were threatened with eviction by the wicked Earl of Clanrickarde; he paid for his Byronesque gesture by serving a term in jail.

Once people visited Galway just to see the Claddagh, a picturesque, if insanitary, fishing village which claimed to be older than the city itself. It was a collection of thatched, whitewashed cottages where the community elected its own king and the women wore magnificent red petticoats. A Claddagh ring, displaying two hands holding a heart surmounted by a crown, served as a wedding ring for brides all over western Ireland and among Irish communities in America. In 1937 the cottages were swept away, to be replaced by nondescript modern council housing, and almost immediately the old traditions began to fade.

Yet a walk around the Claddagh can still be recommended. From its old stone pier the impressive setting of Galway city can be better appreciated: on one side of the bay a long, low coastline stretches out into the Atlantic; on the other, away to the south, lies the eerie, unearthly country of the Burren (to be explored in some detail later). All around here are pleasant walks along river banks and canals, with sea birds gathering and swooping overhead: you might, for instance, suddenly see a cormorant dive and rise into the air again with a wriggling eel in its beak. Certainly it is a rare and moving experience to 'sit and watch the moon rise over Claddagh, and see the sun go down on Galway Bay', as a local song poignantly has it.

Driving south from Galway city, follow the coast road to Clarinbridge, which is famous for its oysters and other shellfish. This is a noted gathering place for gourmets in September when perhaps the finest of all Galway's festivals is staged – the great Oyster Festival.

Dunguaire Castle, near Kinvarra, dating from the sixteenth century but built on the site of the seventh-century palace of King Guaire of Connaught, is worth seeing. Oliver St John Gogarty, one of the great characters of the Irish literary scene, bought it earler this century and had it largely restored to its present romantic appearance.

You are now approaching the Burren ('a rocky place') which is like no other landscape in Europe. It makes inexorable demands on vocabulary because no words quite succeed in defining its appearance. Cromwell's General Ludlow described it as a savage land, yielding 'neither water enough to drown a man, wood enough to hang one, nor soil enough to bury him' – a typical enough, down-to-earth Cromwellian view but one that conveys nothing of the Burren's real character. A lunar landscape of limestone terraces covering 325 square miles of the north-western portion of Co. Clare, it looks from a distance like a sea of pumice rolling down to the Atlantic. Under constantly changing cloud formations it shimmers with colour, pastels and half-tones mixed with sheer bone white, battleship grey and an almost metallic black; I have even seen its desolate expanses turn a golden pink in the evening light.

This gently sloping carboniferous limestone plateau, Europe's youngest landscape, is the result of intense glaciation, while its underground rivers,

Kinvarra, Co. Galway, is a picturesque fishing village on the shores of Galway Bay. This trompe l'œil *mural decorating a shop-front is typical of local enterprise.*

shallow holes, caves, clints, grykes and turloughs are mainly the work of millennia of erosion. Massive erratic limestone blocks dropped by the glaciers as they melted now stand out against the skyline like regiments of cavalry ready to attack. Clints are the smooth limestone pavements that cover most of the area and grykes are the gaping crevices that separate them; both vary enormously in size, with the biggest clint covering 700 square feet and the deepest gryke extending 20 feet. Turloughs are grassy hollows that can fill rapidly with water from subterranean passages, creating lakes which disappear again as rapidly as they form. One cave in this enormous subterranean complex is seven miles long (the impressive Ailwee Cave is open to the public); in others have been found the remains of an African wild cat and an Arctic lemming,

as well as the bones of bears, reindeer and the extinct great Irish elk. This now barren landscape was once covered with pine, hazel and yew but as a result of forest clearance little but hazel remains.

One of the unresolved mysteries of the Burren is what prompted men to settle in such an apparently inhospitable place, yet all the archaeological evidence indicates that it has been inhabited for at least five thousand years. There are, for instance, over sixty prehistoric burial monuments – wedge-shaped gallery graves, cairns and dolmens dating back to the fourth millennium BC; there are also more than five hundred Iron Age forts (cahers or cashels) and innumerable Christian monasteries, round towers, churches and high crosses. Most of the cahers, or ring forts (from the Latin *castrum*), were simply defended domestic sites, but at Ballykinvarga, which has *chevaux de frise* (barriers of stone spikes planted in the ground to obstruct the approach of raiders on horseback), the fort was clearly built for military purposes. This was also true of Cahercommaun, with its triple ramparts, which is sited on the edge of a vertical cliff. On the other hand, Cahermacnaghten, whose enclosure is 100 feet in diameter, was the home of the most famous of Irish law schools. During the twelfth century the Burren was further enriched with three magnificent ecclesiastical sites – Corcomroe Abbey in the north, Kilfenora in the south and Dysert O'Dea, just east of Kilfenora, which are truly sophisticated remnants of an otherwise rough age.

An immense part of the Burren's mystique, however, lies in its extraordinary spectrum of flora. Gazing out at these limestone ridges as one drives along little winding roads, one is constantly startled by the sight of rare and beautiful flowers growing out of the interstices of the rocky pavements. Nowhere else in Europe do Mediterranean and arctic-alpine plants grow side by side, nor do plants that are normally found only on mountain tops live happily at sea level elsewhere. The mystery of how two quite different ecological types, northern and southern, came together like this has never been satisfactorily explained. The best theory offered is that the Lusitanian plants preceded glaciation and remained buried in the tundra when the glaciers arrived from the north, leaving behind them the seeds of arctic plants. Yet why should they continue to flourish so fruitfully? Could it be the high-density light reflecting from the sea on to the naked limestone, or the effects of the Gulf Stream perhaps (snow and frost are hardly known here)? Is it because the limestone absorbs Atlantic warmth and acts as a storage heater? Another mystery is that lime-loving and lime-hating plants here share the same soil. Despite the opinion of General Ludlow, there is no shortage of water: it percolates through rock crevices, flows along horizontal beds and breaks out in small springs throughout the Burren.

The best time to view this magnificent rock garden is late May or early June, when sheet after sheet of the small, delicate peach-yellow flowers of mountain avens spread across the hills, interspersed with vivid blue spring gentians, the gleaming yellow of hoary rockrose, dark blue milkwort and the contrasting shades of the early purple and the Burren orchid. Later in the season (another of the remarkable qualities of the Burren is that there is always something in bloom) come lady's bedstraw, wild thyme, lesser dodder, eyebright, broomrape and the magenta-coloured bloody cranesbill – the list, in fact, is endless, and an inexhaustible delight even to the inexpert eye.

For anyone even vaguely interested in Irish traditional music, Doolin is a mecca. The entire west Clare area is a rich repository of this great cultural legacy and Doolin is recognized as its heartland (although I must advise you to steer clear of the village during the high season, when it is stuffed with trendy young people seeking some Hy-Brasil of their own imagination). The whole district is fascinating, however, teeming with early Christian monuments, prehistoric graves, standing stones and ring forts, and offering splendid views

---

The Burren, Co. Clare. 'A savage land, yielding neither water enough to drown a man, nor a tree to hang him, nor soil enough to bury him'.

of the Aran Islands. In the not-too-distant past it attracted such writers and artists as Synge, Shaw, Augustus John and Dylan Thomas. Doolin is only a stone's throw from the Cliffs of Moher, one of Ireland's great natural wonders: a five-mile length of jutting headlands, they drop sheer to the pounding Atlantic from 700 feet at their highest point, with spindly outriders of dying rock rising as much as 200 feet as they run out to sea.

You have an option now. You can head on to Liscannor, birthplace of John Holland, the inventor of the submarine (a fiercely patriotic Irishman, Holland worked on his ideas in New Jersey with the sole intention of equipping the United States Navy with a weapon guaranteed to overcome British naval supremacy). A better bet is to turn inland and make for Lisdoonvarna, which became a fashionable spa in the eighteenth century. It would be invidious to compare this nondescript, mainly modern town with, say, Bath or Baden Baden, yet its waters reputedly have powerful properties and are said to cure rheumatism. The town's reputation today rests less on its curative powers for the body than on its ability to excite the emotions. It has become, in a sense, to Ireland what St Catherine's Day is to France – an opportunity for unmarried men and women to find a spouse. The tradition began when farmers, having gathered in the harvest, went to the town to rest and recuperate, only to find it filling up with rosy-cheeked farmers' daughters on the look-out to make a match. Until recently, arranged marriages were still customary in rural Ireland; love was rarely considered, and marriage, as with the aristocratic dynasties of old, was a matter of dowries and 'marrying-in' to farms or properties, and was subject to legal contract. The professional matchmakers who became established had an important role to play, bringing together couples they judged to be well-matched. Now it is left

---

The melancholy ruins of the twelfth-century Cistercian Abbey of Corcomroe, in the heart of the Burren.

to the couples who meet there to make their own arrangements, and every September Lisdoonvarna becomes one of the jolliest places on earth.

The hamlet of Kilfenora is, at certain times of the year, surprisingly cosmopolitan; tourists from all over the world crowd into the Burren Display Centre where the geology and topography of the region are expounded in four languages. To me, however, the main object of interest is Kilfenora Cathedral; originally a sixth-century wooden structure, it was rebuilt in stone in the twelfth century. It is not, in fact, for all its antiquity, a distinguished building but it is worth seeing for its twelfth- and thirteenth-century effigies, altar graves and sculptures. Its chief glories, however, are its high crosses: of the five that remain, the twelfth-century Doorty Cross lays claim to be among the three most superb in the country. Standing over 12 feet high, it shows on its best side three bishops and a bird (possibly a symbol of the Holy Spirit), and is further incised with intricate, serpentine Celtic decoration. When they were first erected these high crosses were painted in glowing, primitive colours and must have been even more remarkable.

There are those who find Lemeneagh Castle, east of Kilfenora, rather eerie-looking, almost possessed of a touch of evil; a seventeenth-century building with mullioned and transomed windows built on to a fifteenth-century tower, it stands on rising ground, outlined dramatically against the sky. This was once the home of Maire Rua (Mary of the Red Hair), reputedly Ireland's female Bluebeard, an ugly woman who had no compunction about punishing her servants by hanging them from their hair for half an hour from the castle gargoyles. Her husband, Conor O'Brien, was mortally wounded by the English in 1651, and when stretcher-bearers brought him home the fearsome Maire at first refused to admit them, bellowing out from the ramparts, 'We have no room here for dead men!' Persuaded he was still alive, she finally allowed him in, however, and devotedly nursed him until he died in the early hours. Then, his body scarcely cold, she rode off to Limerick where she offered to marry any English officer there since she believed that by

129

marrying a Protestant she could preserve her castle and lands for her son. A bold Cromwellian cornet called John Cooper took up her offer, but not long afterwards, when helping him to shave, Maire ensured that the razor somehow slipped. She then married another Englishman, who was careless enough to stroll with her on the castle ramparts, off which he somehow fell. A third English husband accepted an invitation from Maire to ride her charger along the Cliffs of Moher. At a whistle from Maire, the horse raised itself on its hind legs and down into the Atlantic went the unfortunate man. Local tradition has it that Maire married twenty-five husbands in total, all of whom seemed to meet a violent fate. She got her comeuppance, however, when she evicted a poor widow from her cottage; bent on revenge, the woman made her way to a group of 'cursing stones' (a feature of this part of Clare) and, turning then towards the castle, cursed Maire that she 'may die roaring with her legs in the air'. A little later, when Maire was out hunting, her horse took fright and threw her into a hollow tree, where she ended up head down and legs in the air; when they found her she was dead.

Killinaboy church boasts two remarkable features. The first is a great cross of Lorraine, constructed as part of the original eleventh to fourteenth-century stone walls; no explanation is yet forthcoming as to why it should have been placed there. The second is more likely to shock delicate susceptibilities, particularly those of anyone who likes to think of a church as the last place to enounter the subject of sex; above the southern doorway is, a 'Sheila-na-Gig'. The name means Sheila-of-the-Breasts, but part of the mystery of these figures, which are to be seen all over Ireland, is that no breasts are shown. Instead, the figures are alarmingly obscene representations of a nude woman, with legs wide open, exposing her genitals. These sculptures, as here at Killinaboy, are always found in sacred places but the only thing known about them for certain is that they are not pagan fertility symbols. They all date from after the Norman Conquest, when Ireland had been Christian for many centuries. The likeliest explanation for their appearance in such unexpected places is that, since female genitals are seen as the very source of life, they are thought to ward off the devil, prevent famine and floods, stop aggression and even cure sickness; certainly European medieval superstitious tradition would lend credence to this theory.

Kilmacduagh is famous for its saint, Colman MacDuagh, a kinsman of the King Guaire who built the original Dunguaire Castle. The village has a fourteenth to fifteenth-century cathedral, which contains sixteenth-century O'Shaughnessy tombs. Nearby are the ruins of O'Heyne's Abbey, whose chancel arch and windows in the Irish romanesque style date from 1266, and a magnificent round tower which leans more than two feet from the perpendicular.

By the time you reach Gort (ancestral home of Lord Gort VC, who commanded the British Army during Hitler's 1940 blitzkrieg), you have re-entered Co. Galway and are into a richer countryside, where the great Irish literary revival of the *fin de siècle* had its inception. Coole Park was in those days the home of Lady Augusta Gregory, scion of an old Cromwellian family; widowed shortly after her marriage, she threw herself into the task of gathering up all the ancient Celtic myths and folklore of the region. Assisted in her search by Yeats, she collected these ancient tales into books and plays in Irish, and suddenly she found herself plunged, both as patroness and participator, into that cultural fever which saw the establishment of the Abbey Theatre and stimulated a literature that became world famous. Her lovely estate inspired Yeats, a frequent visitor, to write several fine pieces there, among them 'The Wild Swans at Coole', whose first verse ends with the lines:

Upon the brimming water among the stones
are nine-and-fifty swans.

The Cliffs of Moher, Co. Clare. These precipitous sandstone cliffs, almost 700 ft high and stretching for five miles, provide spectacular views of the Atlantic crashing below.

'Coole Park, 1929' was his elegy for the life there that had already gone:

When all those rooms and passages are gone,
When nettles wave upon a shapeless mound
And saplings root among the broken stone . . .

Many of the great cultural figures of the day visited Coole, among them Bernard Shaw, J. M. Synge, Augustus John, John Masefield, Katherine Tynan, Sean O'Casey, Douglas Hyde (founder of the Gaelic League), Violet Martin (co-author, under her pseudonym of Martin Ross, of the 'Irish R.M.' books) and many others. They carved their initials on a great copper beech tree, known now as the Autograph Tree, which still stands in the grounds. Coole House itself has long since disappeared. In 1927 Lady Gregory realized that because of mounting debts she could no longer keep the estate and sold it to the Irish Forestry Commission; she retained permission, however, to continue to reside there, which she did until her death in 1932. The Irish Government, which for many years showed a marked disinclination to preserve the big houses of the old Ascendancy class (some of its members had even helped to burn them down), allowed it to deteriorate, and finally in 1941 it was demolished.

If your time allows and you are interested in Ireland's pre-Norman past, I recommend that you now strike inland some thirty-five miles to see what is, in my opinion, one of the most haunting sites in Ireland, the melancholy ruins of the famed monastery of Clonmacnoise in Co. Offaly. Magnificently set in a sylvan bend of the Shannon, the longest natural waterway in the British Isles, this ancient, walled monastic site is best approached by boat along the river from Athlone, so that its antique graves, early Christian buildings, round towers and high crosses rise majestically out of the morning mists that cloud in across the water. But from whichever direction you approach it, it is a beautiful and timeless place.

Founded by St Ciaran in 545, it became the most celebrated religious foundation in Ireland. As the epicentre of Irish art and literature, it had no rival and its status was that of a university. In their scriptoria the monks produced some of the earliest vernacular Irish histories, including the Book of the Dun Cow (now in the Bodleian Library, Oxford) and the Annals of Tighernach. Two intellectual giants studied here. The first was Alcuin, an Englishman who took the learning of Clonmacnoise to the court of Charlemagne, where he came to be acknowledged as the greatest scholar in Western Europe. The second was an Irishman, John Scotus Erigena, a philosopher-theologian who became chief professor at the Palace School of Charles the Bald; a daring Neoplatonist, whose teachings on free will and original sin are still studied, he was a master of Latin and Greek when even emperors could not write their names.

Clonmacnoise has suffered much from assault. It was burned thirteen times and sacked eight times by the Vikings (in 884 the notorious Turgesius burned down the monastery after his wife, Ota, had desecrated the main altar by dancing on it lasciviously and expounding pagan teachings). It was attacked thirty-three times between 832 and 1204 before being reduced to an utter ruin by the English in 1552 when, it was claimed, 'not a bell, large or small or an image, or an altar, or a book or a gem, or even a glass in a window were left'. What restoration had been accomplished was again destroyed a hundred years later when Cromwell actually cannonaded the site. O'Rourke's Tower, which had been damaged by lightning centuries earlier, had a few more stones knocked out of it in the attack but still stands 60 feet tall. There is a second, largely undamaged tower on the site, called MacCarthy's Tower, which rises to 56 feet. In the space available I can only mention a few other points of interest. Many Irish kings were buried here and at the causeway near the entrance is an assembly of sixth to eleventh-century grave slabs that are well worth seeing. There are also

Lemeneagh Castle, Co. Clare, was the home of the infamous Maire Rua, a female Bluebeard who ran through several husbands before dying a violent death.

three high crosses; one – the Cross of the Scriptures – which stands just outside the ruined cathedral is among the best in the country. The cathedral itself, which has a splendid twelfth-century romanesque doorway, contains the grave of Roderick (or Rory) O'Connor, the last high king of Ireland. St Ciaran himself is believed to lie under the floor of the church known as Tempall Ciaran. Some five hundred yards east of the main settlement stands the tenth-century Nun's Church, whose entrance door and chancel arch were magnificently decorated by the pathetic Dervorgilla, Ireland's Helen of Troy.

From Clonmacnoise turn north through Athlone (birthplace of the tenor John MacCormack), drive on through Roscommon town (which has the remains of a thirteenth-century Norman castle) and stop briefly at Castlerea. You might find the countryside around here dull compared with the coast, for the interior of Ireland, which includes the immense and dreary Bog of Allen, is not dramatic countryside despite the Shannon and its necklace of lakes. However, it is worth visiting Clonalis House, an Italianate mansion occupied by the descendants of King Rory O'Connor. The family, whose genealogical table is on view (it traces their ancestry back to 1352 BC), have lived on the same land since AD 75. There are many delightful artefacts in the house, and among the exhibits displayed in its small museum is the harp of blind Turlough O'Carolan, last of the great Irish harpists, whose music was noted down for posterity at the Belfast Harp Festival of 1792.

Here you are only a few miles from a royal residence of the Iron Age that once surpassed even the glory of Tara. Cruachan was the ancient palace of Queen Maeve, goddess-wife of King Ailill and Amazonian adversary of the great warrior champion Cuchulainn. Sadly, there is little to see – the palace itself, which once had five concentric ramparts, is now little more

than a series of grass-grown mounds – but this is a place of deep significance: a track leads to Roilig na Ríogh, the royal burial ground where three of the queens of the Tuatha de Danaan tribe who have given their names to Ireland – Eriu (or Eire), Banba and Fodla – are buried along with many kings. On a mound not far from here stands a solitary upright pillar of glaring red sandstone – this in a land of limestone – which marks the grave of Daithí, last pagan high king of Ireland and the Scottic race. A remarkable leader, Daithí extended Scottic conquests through many parts of eastern Britain and as far as the English Channel before leading an army through France to Piedmont. There he languished for seven months at the Castle of Sales, studying classical manuscripts and observing the disintegration of the Western Empire. He was killed by lightning at the foot of the Alps in about AD 428, and his body was carried on a litter of shields through France, southern Britain and Caledonia to its last resting place here.

It was at Cruachan that Maeve and her husband plotted the disastrous Cattle Raid of Cooley (Taín Bó Cuailgne) the subject of the greatest of all Irish epic tales, when the forces of Connaught invaded Ulster to capture the prized Brown Bull of Cooley and were harried and harassed the whole way, single-handed, by Cuchulainn. In this great work Irish life as it was before Christ is vividly recreated.

Your road now turns west through Ballyhaunis. If you are of a religious nature you might like to diverge to Knock, now an important pilgrimage site where the Virgin is alleged to have manifested herself in 1879; if not, carry on through Claremorris and along the delightful shores of Lough Carra to Lough Mask, whose waters reflect their dramatic purple backdrop of the Partry Mountains. Head for Cong Abbey, which lies between Lough Mask and Lough Corrib (Ireland's second largest lake); an Augustinian establishment founded by King Turlough O'Connor in 1128, its architecture blends Irish romanesque and gothic. The Cross of Cong, made nearby in Co. Roscommon, is among Ireland's greatest treasures and was presented to the abbey by King Rory O'Connor when he retired

A doorway at Clonmacnoise, Co. Offaly, the most majestic of early Christian monasteries. Some of the greatest early medieval scholars were taught here.

to live out his days here after the Norman Conquest. A short distance away stands Ashford Castle, a castellated Victorian affair whose origins lie in the thirteenth century; formerly the home of Lord Ardilaun, head of the Guinness family, it is now a luxury hotel and a superb base for exploring the local countryside.

This whole area is a spur to the imagination. Just south-east of Tuam, for instance, lies Castle Hackett demesne where you will see a hill 600 feet high. This, according to song and story, is the seat of Finbarr, king of the fairies of Connacht who once fought a fierce battle here against the invading fairies of Munster. North-east of Cong lies the Plain of Moytura, where the invading Tuatha de Danaan overcame the Firbolgs, another of the ancient races of Ireland, after a four-day battle, to become rulers of the island. Two great cairns of heaped stones, one 60 feet high and both more than three thousand years old, were investigated in the last century by Sir William Wilde who lived at nearby Moytura House (Oscar himself spent most of his boyhood holidays there). Sir William identified one heap, which concealed a passage grave, as that of the grave of Eochy, king of the Firbolgs. The second, he surmised, had been raised by the Firbolgs in the course of the battle, each stone being placed, according to custom, to mark the death of an enemy. Ireland would hardly be Ireland, of course, if there were not ghostly manifestations associated with these memorials, and it is said that hundreds of men have been seen marching in columns towards these cairns and have then simply vanished into the ground.

It is easy to transport yourself back in time in this landscape. A step or two into woodland near Lough Carra brings you into a primeval world of ferns and fallen trees smothered in moss and lichen. Where the sun manages to penetrate the tree cover are thickets ablaze with wild strawberry flowers, the white stars of

Lough Corrib, Co. Galway, Ireland's second largest lake. Dotted with beautiful islets, it is an angler's paradise, providing the best free fishing in the British Isles.

the spindle-tree, the cool blue of speedwell and the yellow of cinquefoil, with wild thyme and sweet briar scenting the air. On Lough Carra itself you will see crannogs – curious round huts built on wooden piles – which were erected in prehistoric times and have yielded up harps, finely wrought brooches, combs, beautifully decorated swords and scabbards, delicate drinking cups and other ornaments.

The focal points of interest in this area are loughs Corrib and Mask, which are now accessible to large numbers of fishermen from the European mainland by means of Knock international airport. The fishing is, of course, superb though no one is guaranteed a catch.

West of Cong you enter Connemara, which is not in fact a county, as many people suppose, but a coastal district. Though it has no clear boundaries, it can be said roughly to extend northwards from Bertraghboy Bay in Galway to Killary Harbour in Mayo, and from the Atlantic in the west to Joyce Country in the east. Here you will find yourself plunged into one of the wildest and most beautiful, if austerely beautiful, landscapes in the world. In Connemara you leave behind the fertile limestone acres of east Galway for a dramatic land of granite and volcanic debris, deep glens and rhapsodic tarns, cliffs and mountains and mountain lakes and lake islands. The soft air is full of the sound of water cascading between stones. Black cattle contentedly chew the cud in tiny fields enclosed by dry-stone walls, which in the strange light that sometimes pervades this place can look like a string of pearls. There is the odd donkey on the road. Sods of turf are stacked up to dry against house walls. Roads meander among small lakes bordered by moss- and lichen-covered boulders of all shapes and sizes, pebbles glinting with quartz and slate-green antique rocks, like stranded prehistoric sea monsters. Wild swans glide on the waters – true wild swans these which, unlike the domesticated English swan, are not mute but sing like women humming a mournful song. Limpid pools shimmer in the dark, purplish-brown bogs. You discover a coastline indented with huge scythes and crescents of almost opalescent sand, and headlands breaking off into small rocky islands linked together far out into the Atlantic as though someone had tried to build a causeway to America. Brooding over the whole region are the Maamturk Mountains and the peaks called the Twelve Bens of Connemara.

As you make for Leenane you first pass through the district known as Joyce Country after a Welsh family who settled here in the thirteenth century. There are lakes to enchant you on your way, including beautiful, lonely Lough Nafooey; the Sheeffry Hills rise to your right and to your left loom up the great shadows of the Maamturks and behind them the Bens. Leenane, spectacularly placed near the head of Killary Harbour, is dominated by the Devil's Mountain (about 2000 feet high), around which many wild stories and superstitions have gathered. Killary Harbour is, in fact, a misnomer as this is the most impressive fiord in Ireland, a ten-mile-long tongue of Atlantic water cutting deep through high mountains which rise sheer on either side. Perhaps the most impressive sight in the area is the entrance to the fiord, where the Mweelrea Mountains drop almost sheer for 2500 feet.

Heading towards Clifden, with the Connemara National Park on your left, you will glimpse across a silken lake one of Galway's most romantic sights, Kylemore Abbey, a turreted, fairytale affair in a lush setting of rhododendron and fuchsia. Sadly, the castle is a phoney, built by a Liverpool millionaire in the late nineteenth century; it is now used by the Benedictine nuns of Ypres as a school. Its great trophy, proudly exhibited in the great hall, is a British flag captured by the Irish Brigade of the French royal army at Fontenoy.

Turn off to the right at Letterfrack, on a side road to Tully Cross and Renvyle. Renvyle House, now a hotel, was originally the property of the Blake family and was later bought by Oliver St John Gogarty, who entertained many of the great cultural figures of the day here. Augustus John, who called the area 'the most

---

Killary Harbour, Co. Galway, is not a harbour at all, but the drowned valley of the River Erriff, creating a dramatic fiord-like inlet ten miles long.

beautiful landscape in the world', painted several pictures nearby. Shaw and Joyce were both visitors to Renvyle while Yeats, uneasy because 'of the spirits' (there had been a murder here), dabbled in mystic ceremonies and held occasional seances in the house. When I last visited it the hotel was still reputedly haunted – not by a Blake but by a figure said to resemble Yeats himself.

Six miles off shore lies Inishbofin (Island of the White Cow) where the great St Colman, former Abbot of Lindisfarne, founded a monastery for English and Irish monks. He retreated here after he had lost the debate at Whitby in 664 over the alignment of the Celtic Church with Rome. Bede tells us that after a while the English and Irish monks failed to get on together, the Irish preferring to enjoy themselves in their spare time while the English concentrated on improving their farms and gardens. In the end Colman moved his establishment to Mayo, which as a result became known as 'Mayo of the Saxons', and the new foundation gained such fame that it elicited the personal praise of Charlemagne himself.

There are so many gorgeous sights in Connemara that I can mention only a few. Clifden, the nominal capital, is an undistinguished town in a superb setting. The coastal road from here will take you to a desolate spread of bogland where Alcock and Brown crash-landed in June 1919 after the first transatlantic flight in history. Continue round this superb stretch of coast, with its islands, bays and beaches, to Roundstone, a cluster of whitewashed houses overlooking Bertragh-boy Bay, where lobsters, crabs, trout and other delicacies are in plentiful supply. Just above the village rises high ground called Errisbeg from whose 1000-foot summit you can see all Connemara, the innumerable islands off shore and even the distant mountains of Kerry.

Kylemore Abbey, Connemara, seen across one of its lakes. Despite its ancient appearance it was in fact built in the nineteenth century, on reclaimed bogland.

Ballynahinch Castle, situated beside a lake of the same name, is now a hotel in a glorious setting. It once belonged to the O'Flahertys but was seized in Elizabethan times by Sir Richard Bingham, President of Connacht and the detested foe of Red Hugh O'Donnell. It passed to the Martin family whose best-known member, Colonel Richard Martin, founded the RSPCA and became known as 'Humanity Dick'.

Taking the coast road back to Galway, you will find a track at Rosmuck leading to the thatched cottage where Pearse, leader of the 1916 Insurrection, came to study Irish (this is a Gaeltacht area), translated Irish poetry into English and wrote plays and poems in the Irish language. The little cottage, which is open to the public, is furnished as it was when he was here. From Rosmuck it is an enchanting trip back through Inverin and Spiddal, although the sight of ugly modern bungalows may diminish your pleasure. These monstrosities are undoubtedly more convenient for the people who have to live in them than the whitewashed cottages of old but they betray a sad poverty of imagination in a country which needs to find its own architectural expression, if only in domestic matters.

What once drew people to the Aran Islands as though to some Shangri-La was its primitive style of life, the strange compelling beauty of its limestone plateaus, the vertiginous 400-foot cliffs, the constant thunder of the ocean, the countless tombs, early churches and high crosses, and such prehistoric fortresses as Dun Aengus which has been described as 'the most magnificent barbaric monument in Europe'. This last is the object of endless speculation: how old is it? Which of the races of Ireland built it? Why was it built here at all? Who were the putative invaders? Awesome and mysterious, it is perched perilously on the edge of a 300-foot cliff which drops sheer to the Atlantic on the west coast of Inishmore, the largest island in the group. It consists of three lines of ramparts, the outer one enclosing in total some eleven acres, and is fronted on the landward side by impressive *chevaux de frise*. Altogether there are five great prehistoric forts scattered across the three islands, Inishmore, Inishmaan and Inisheer.

The Aran Islands are still sometimes called Ara of the Saints for it was on Inishmore that St Enda built Ireland's first monastery, from which the whole hermitical idea spread to the rest of the country. No fewer than 125 other 'saints' (the word originally meant teachers or learned men) attended his burial.

These strange islands first entered modern Irish affections when Synge, then living in Paris, was advised by Yeats, 'Give up Paris. Go to the Aran Islands. Live there as if you were one of the people themselves; express a life that has never found expression.' Taking his advice, Synge lodged in a cottage on Inishmaan. There he studied the Irish language and particularly the unusual Hiberno-English dialect of the people, whose beautiful speech rhythms he revealed to the world in *Riders to the Sea* and *The Playboy of the Western World*.

Although it is likely that many islanders descend from neolithic inhabitants, a large number are actually descendants of an English Elizabethan garrison, which was further reinforced during Cromwellian times. Aran men are said to look conspicuously different from other natives of Ireland's West, and this may be because the most 'Irish' part of Ireland was, in fact, an English colony – speaking Irish, of course. But then nothing on the islands is quite straightforward: on Inisheer, for example, the water from one well will only boil when all the other wells have gone dry.

Even the look of the islands is decidedly strange; from the air Inishmore looks almost like an abstract painting, with its small, geometric fields enclosed by dry-stone walls, laboriously built up out of the limestone rock (the ancient stone forts have been plundered in the same way as were the ruins of classical Rome). Life on the Aran Islands is no longer lived in quite the primitive form that has characterized it for millennia, and tourism and fishing now provide

---

Roundstone Harbour, Connemara, arguably the prettiest on the western coast. It was constructed in the 1820s by a Scotch engineer who settled it with Scottish fishermen.

the Inishmore islanders with an excellent living (be warned, indeed; you will be taken aback at the cost of everything). Locally made currachs similar to those used by St Brendan, which are used to fish for oil-bearing basking sharks, now cost £500 and are equipped with outboard motors. On Inishmaan, where tourism has made less of an impact, some women still sport the traditional red shawls and the men a tam-o'-shanter-style hat of grey tweed with a big bobble on top. But consumerism, which has not by any means left Ireland unscathed, has also attacked the islands and much is changed. A sign of the times is that the islands now actually import potatoes – traditionally their own greatest crop – from the Netherlands. Aran potatoes, grown in the soil created by spreading sand and seaweed in alternate layers on the bare rock pavements, were claimed by connoisseurs to be among the most delicious anywhere.

There are two principal ways of reaching the Aran Islands: ferries run regularly from the mainland and nowadays there is also an air service from Galway to Inishmore. The real problem is the weather; this can sour with dramatic suddenness and visitors can be stranded for several days, particularly on the two smaller islands of Inishmaan and Inisheer.

One of the most enduring legends connected with the islands concerns Hy-Brasil, the Isle of the Blest. For centuries men believed in an enchanted island lying out to the west and, indeed, such an island was marked on maritime maps until the eighteenth century. This mirage has mocked men down through the ages, persuading them they have seen an aspect of heaven; the longing for paradise that it represents was never better expressed than in the verses of Gerald Griffin:

On the ocean that hollows the rocks where ye dwell,
A shadowy land has appear'd, as they tell;
Men thought it a region of sunshine and rest,
And they called it Hy-Brasail – the Isle of the Blest
And from year unto year, on the ocean's blue rim
The beautiful spectre showed lovely and dim;
The gold clouds curtain'd the deep where it lay,
And it looked like an Eden, away, far away.

143

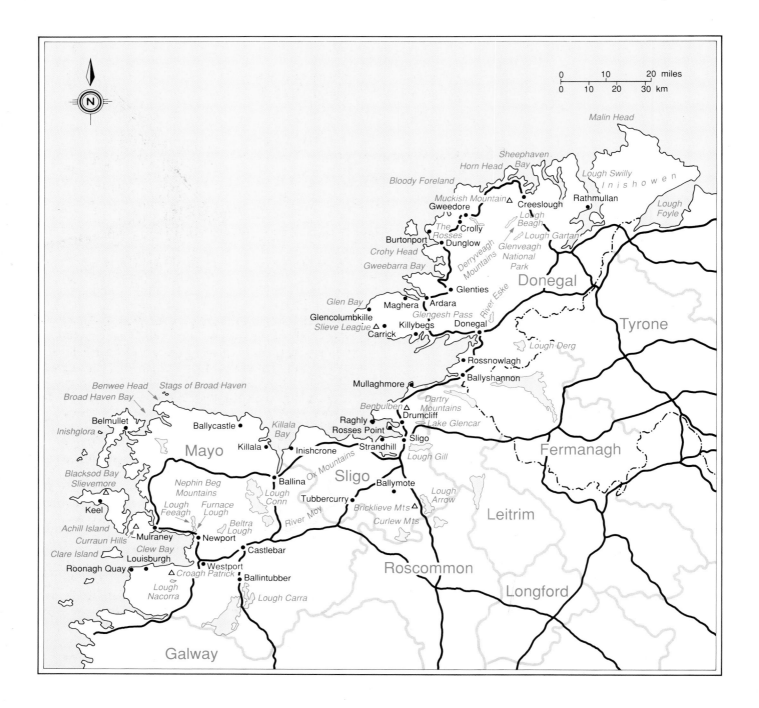

5
Westport and the North-West

Westport – Croagh Patrick – Clare Island – Ballintubber

Castlebar – Achill Island – Belmullet – Killala – Sligo

Ballymote – Drumcliff – Donegal Town – Glencolumbkille

Glenties – The Rosses – Glenveagh National Park

Horn Head – Inishowen

I confess to an immense liking for Westport. Its hinterland consists of some of the remotest and bleakest scenery in Europe, and it is almost startling to find such a finely wrought town amid a wilderness of boulder-strewn, scarcely inhabited countryside perched out here on the Atlantic verge.

Westport, elegantly designed by James Wyatt in the late eighteenth century for Peter Browne, second Earl of Altamont, is embellished with two splendid set pieces, the Octagon and the Mall. The Octagon is the unusually shaped main square, which is open to allow street entrances on three sides. The Mall, running through the lower town, gives the place its air of being a Low Countries transplant. The River Carrowbeg has been canalized here and lined with tall sycamore and lime trees; crossed by a fine eighteenth-century bridge, it is flanked by good Georgian houses, one of which has an unusual five-bay window.

Peter Browne, a member of the derided Ascendancy class was, in fact, an outstanding benefactor of the region and a shining example of a social order which, under better circumstances, might have created a more prosperous and less quarrelsome Ireland. He introduced modern agricultural methods to the Westport area, established a linen industry in the town and built some elegant warehouses (these still stand beside the excellent harbour which he also constructed), and he provided good houses for his weavers, who were given looms and money to buy yarn. Sadly, the Union with Britain in 1801 destroyed the linen venture since hand looms were unable to compete with England's new spinning-jennies.

James Wyatt had initially been engaged by Peter Browne to complete the interiors of Westport House, a pale grey limestone building designed in the 1730s by Richard Castle, which lies a short distance outside the town. Now the seat of the Marquess of Sligo, it was built on the site of an old O'Malley castle belonging to John Browne, a descendant of Henry VIII's Master of Horse. (Browne's wife was a great, great granddaughter of Grace O'Malley, the Gaelic queen of Connacht in Elizabethan times and the most notable pirate in Irish history.) Purists may easily feel disappointed in Westport House because it has been over-commercialized. Yet nothing can dim the lustre of its treasures: a magnificent barrel ceiling by Castle in the front hall; a glorious staircase in gleaming white Sicilian marble; Rubens' *The Holy Family*; Wyatt's

masterly, if austere, dining room; the head of an Irish elk dug out of a bog a hundred and fifty years ago and dating back over ten thousand years; J. M. Synge's violin; a superb collection of eighteenth-century Irish landscapes by James O'Connor; a rare collection of early English and Irish silver and eighteenth-century Waterford glass; and the Flag of the Mayo Legion, made by Frenchwomen and brought to Ireland by General Humbert when the French landed at Killala in 1798 to assist the Irish Rebellion.

The third Earl of Altamont, who later became the first Marquess of Sligo, was a friend of Byron's. Caught up in the Romantic movement, he went to Greece searching for antiquities for the house. He swam with Byron off Piraeus and rode overland with him to Corinth but finally succumbed to homesickness and returned to Ireland. The eighteenth-century fishing lodge of Delphi on Fin Lough, north of Killary, owes its name to his enthusiasm for Greece.

Leaving Westport, now head west along a coastline that will allow you a stunning panorama of Clew Bay with its three hundred and sixty-five islands. Your objective is Croagh Patrick, a 2510-foot quartz-veined cone of a mountain where St Patrick is said to have feasted for forty days in AD 441.

Even today, in the high-tide of consumerism, sixty thousand pilgrims come every year on the last Sunday in July to make the pilgrimage to the summit of the 'holy mountain'. Once it was considered the done thing to climb in one's bare feet; today a few older pilgrims still subject themselves to this torture but the younger generation are said to favour trainers. If you feel like making the climb, even if not for a religious purpose, you will be well rewarded by the magnificent views from the top.

Traditionally, it was from here that Patrick banished snakes from Ireland, flinging a bell down the

James Wyatt's dining-room at Westport House is considered to be one of his masterpieces.

slope time after time in order to encourage all the repellent creatures in Ireland to follow the noise and throw themselves after it like lemmings. Spirits dutifully returned the bell to the saint each time. He was attacked by demons, including Corra, mother of the Devil, but flung them into a deep hollow at the bottom of the mountain with such force that water burst forth and created Lough na Corra.

Scientists do not, of course, subscribe to the idea that Patrick's exertions were in any way responsible for protecting Ireland from venomous reptiles. Their theory is that when the ice retreated about nine thousand years ago, the seas rose rapidly all round Ireland, cutting it off from Britain which itself remained attached to the Continent. By the time the snakes managed to make their way up to Britain's western coast, the Irish sea had formed to stop them.

Westport House, Co. Mayo, seat of the marquesses of Sligo. It was designed by Richard Castle in 1731 with additions by Thomas Ivory.

147

A fairly gentle slope leads up from Murrisk Abbey to the first 'station' where pilgrims make seven praying circuits round a cairn of stones. The climb now becomes harder and continues hard to the summit. There mass is held, followed by fifteen praying circuits round a little chapel and seven round St Patrick's Bed, a pile of stones where the saint is said to have slept. The last station is St Patrick's Garden, an enclosure to the west of the summit containing three tumuli, around each of which pilgrims must walk seven times before circling the perimeter seven times.

From Croagh Patrick, continue west to Louisburg and out to Roonagh Quay, where you have the option of simply enjoying a superb view or taking a boat out to Clare Island, once Grace O'Malley's headquarters. Daughter of an O'Malley chieftain, Grace built up her own formidable army and navy, handling her fleet so expertly that she frequently put English ships to flight or captured them. To ensure the safety of her vessels, she passed their mooring cables through the windows of her castle, that of the fastest being attached to her own bedpost. A tough woman of few scruples, she first showed her mettle after her first husband, whom she had saved from drowning, was killed in an ambush. She calmly bided her time before taking her revenge and then attacked the enemy when they were at their most vulnerable, slaughtered all who had taken part in the attack and took over their castle. Her second marriage, to Sir Richard Burke, was an astonishing example of deceit and treachery on her part: a condition of the marriage was that if either party considered it was not working during the course of the first year, they could say 'I dismiss you' and that would be that. When the conditional year was up Grace said the words, and not only turned Burke out of the matrimonial home but seized all his other castles and properties as well. Governor Bingham of Connacht decided to hang her for this deception, calling her 'a notable traitor and nurse of all rebellions', but was induced to let her go free when she handed over her son-in-law as hostage. She was eventually invited to London to meet Queen Elizabeth. True to her nature, Grace, who was very tall, held out her hand a little higher than the queen's so that Elizabeth had to raise her own. In spite of this, tradition has it that Elizabeth then said, 'I'd like to make you a countess', to which Grace replied, 'You can't do that! Am I not a queen already, the same as yourself!'

Grace's arrogance and ruthlessness stemmed from the O'Malleys on Clare Island, particularly when survivors of an Armada shipwreck staggered ashore in September 1588. All along the Irish coast that stormy autumn, Armada ships were lost in horrendous circumstances; altogether twenty-six foundered on Ireland's west coast, many more than suffered at the hands of Drake and his fellows. In some instances the Irish chieftains helped the survivors and enabled them to reach safety through Scotland, but the O'Malleys, keen to ingratiate themselves with Governor Bingham, slaughtered all who came ashore nearby.

From this scene of ancient carnage you may find it a relief to backtrack to Westport and thence south-east to the abbey of Ballintubber, where mass has been offered, without a break, for seven hundred and fifty years. Even in penal times, when mass was forbidden, the local people gathered in the precincts of their roofless church. Patrick founded the original church, in its beautiful setting on the shores of Lough Carra, on his return from his forty days on Croagh Patrick, and used the nearby well to baptize converts. In 1216 the then Gaelic king of Connacht, Cathal Mór O'Connor ('of the wine-red hand') founded a new church on the site; the present structure is the only one in Ireland that was founded by an Irish king and is still in use. An ancient track, said to have been beaten out by Patrick on his way to the holy mountain, is still open.

Ballintubber survived the Dissolution because of its sheer remoteness. In Henry VIII's time much of Ireland remained a fastness that the English rarely penetrated, and then at their peril. The Cromwellians, however, were a more pertinacious crew, who duly sought out

Croagh Patrick, Ireland's holy mountain, seen across the vast expanse of Clew Bay at sunrise.

the abbey and then wrecked it. Restoration began in the nineteenth century. Its architecture is worth studying because it illustrates the transition from Irish Romanesque to gothic, and its interior is impressive for its atmosphere of sober austerity. The west doorway, dating from the fifteenth century, is also of interest.

Castlebar is Mayo's county town, but has little to commend it to the traveller beyond a certain notoriety arising from the fact that its owner is the missing Lord Lucan. It was also here that a small French force under General Humbert, aided by some hopeful Irish rebels, put to flight a British army under General Lake in an episode known sardonically as 'The Races at Castlebar' for the speed at which the British ran away.

By some glorious oversight the Mayo coast north of Westport has been generally ignored by the package tour industry, and for this reason alone is attractive to anyone who wishes to relish the glories of unspoiled scenery. The loughs to the north-east of Clew Bay — Beltra, Furnace, Feeagh and particularly Conn — which are all within easy reach of Westport, offer magnificent salmon and trout fishing. The superb mountains of the Nephin Beg range, peaking at 2646 feet, extend north-westwards, often shrouded in mist or rain.

I find the road up through Newport (home of the Kelly family, which produced Princess Grace of Monaco) and Mulranney towards Achill Island one of the most soul-refreshing of any in Ireland. Just past Newport you can detour slightly towards the sea, to Rockfleet Castle, one of the houses that Grace O'Malley filched so deceitfully from her second husband. Mulranney deserves the epithet 'pretty' for it is a riot of fuchsia, rhododendron and Mediterranean heath while facing it westwards are the juniper-clad Curraun hills on the peninsula of the same name. Then suddenly you are on Achill Island. Achill is the largest of Ireland's off-shore islands and is separated from the

Ballintubber Abbey, Co. Mayo, founded in 1216, was destroyed by Cromwell but mass continued to be held in the ruins. The abbey has now been splendidly restored.

Clew Bay, Co. Mayo, is one of western Ireland's greatest sights. Fifteen miles long and six miles in width, it is dotted with small islands.

mainland by Achill Sound, a stretch of water a mere twenty yards wide which has now been bridged so that you are on the island almost without realizing it.

The contrast with the country through which you have been travelling is marked, not so much because the contours of the landscape are very different as because this is a traditional Irish holiday resort, a tourist trade having been well-established here since

the Second World War. The weather can be harsh, but people come for the beaches and the magnificent views. Although there is an 'Atlantic Drive', the island is best explored on foot if you have the time and energy. Inland you will be faced with expanses of bogland and mountainous humps but you will also find ancient cairns, dolmens, standing stones and standing circles. The island's highest point is Slievemore on the north coast, a daunting pile of quartzite and mica 2204 feet high but worth the climb. Burrowing back into the mountain are the Seal Caves which can be visited only by boat. Some distance to the west lies Croaghaun, which falls almost sheer from its summit at 2192 feet to a four-mile stretch of precipices, the highest sea-cliffs in the British Isles.

The island has a very good beach at Keel, the chief resort, where two miles of unpolluted sands end at the fantastical Cathedral Rocks, where the cliffs have been eroded by the sea to produce magical columns and caves. These are really an extension of the awe-inspiring Meenaun Cliffs, which fall over 800 feet.

Until quite recently the islanders lived in poverty, their income largely consisting of remittances from overseas relatives. Today tourism and the shark-fishing industry allow them modest prosperity. You may be surprised to spot dorsal fins in the sea even as Irish holidaymakers bathe happily from nearby beaches but the majority of these sharks are of the basking variety who live on plankton, and their valuable oil makes them the prey rather than the predators of humans. (Among the thirty-five varieties of fish caught in Blacksod Bay, that enormous inlet to the north of Achill, is the blue shark, which is far from harmless; yet amazingly, there are no records of bathers being attacked by sharks along Ireland's west coast.)

A cottage at Mulranney, Co. Mayo. These traditional rural dwellings are now being supplanted by suburban-style bungalows.

Return to the mainland now and take the road running north from Mulranney along Bellacragher Bay, with the pounding sea to your left and the Nephin Beg range to your right. In response to the constantly shifting patterns, dramatic shafts of sunlight, banks of mist and sudden showers, the mountains change colour like chameleons. Close up they are great green ridges scattered with tufted browns, pearly cascades of water washing down their sides, yet they often take on an intense blue, deepening to dark purple which somehow or other enhances the loneliness and romanticism of this remote region. Stretching northwards, seemingly to infinity, is the great Bog of Erris, more than two hundred square miles of utter emptiness. Yet from Cromwell's time until the Famine these western lands held the bulk of the Irish population: in 1841 Co. Mayo supported, though at subsistence level, 475 people for every acre of arable land.

Only a short distance ahead lies the stretch of coast where Humbert and his French revolutionary expedition came ashore, and where, only two centuries earlier, an almost equal danger to the English interest had arisen. On 7 September 1588, driven off course by storms and with maritime maps that were absurdly inaccurate, *La Rata Encorado*, flagship of the Armada's second-in-command, Don Alfonso de Levya, was wrecked in Blacksod Bay. Having rescued the ship's treasure, Don Alfonso and his troops managed to find shelter in the ruins of an old castle where he was joined by the survivors of a second ship which had also foundered. He had more than a thousand superb fighting men under his command, abundant treasure to pay for goods and services, and the opportunity, if only he had known it, of rousing the Irish clans and possibly throwing the English out of Ireland altogether (England had only token forces in the island at the time and they had been thrown into panic by the approach of the Armada). Although he was entertained by the chief of the O'Rourkes at Dromahair Castle, Don Alfonso does not appear to have been provided with this intelligence. Instead, with O'Rourke's assistance, he managed to refloat one of his damaged ships and set off northwards, hoping to reach Scotland, then an

independent country. At the Donegal coast they discovered another great ship, the *Girona*, aground but in much better shape than their own vessel. Transferring all his men and treasure to the *Girona*, Don Alfonso limped off for Scotland. Storm again struck and the ship was driven on the rocks near Dunluce Castle, the seat of Sorley Boy, chief of the MacDonnells, in Co. Antrim. As many men as possible were rescued but Don Alfonso was not among the survivors. Within the last few decades sub-aqua exploration has uncovered the wreck, and much of its armament and gold treasure has been raised to the surface and now rests in the Ulster Museum in Belfast. For a moment, it is clear, England and Elizabeth's fate had lain in the hands of those desperate men in Blacksod Bay.

Belmullet sits on a narrow isthmus between the mainland and the Mullet Peninsula, surrounded by the great spaces of Blacksod and Broad Haven bays. The whole peninsula is wild and windswept, and its desolate, treeless countryside has never attracted me, though there are acres of sand dunes and many excellent beaches with antiquities to be discovered everywhere; an ancient fort, Doonamo, a smaller version of Dun Aengus, on the north-west coast is worth visiting. Here, too, is the last Irish nesting place of the great phalarope. Off shore to the west is the island of Inishglora where St Brendan founded a monastery. The air of this island is reputed to be remarkable in that it acts as a preservative: the Book of Ballymote, written in about 1400, records that 'bodies brought here do not rot. Nails and hair grow and everyone recognizes his father and grandfather for a long time after death.'

The waters around Inishglora are also the setting for the denouement of one of the most beautiful and tender tales in all Celtic literature – the story of the Children of Lir (pronounced Leer). Lir was a divinity of the Tuatha de Danaan, who had a daughter, Fionnuala, and three sons by his first wife; when he remarried their stepmother became jealous and decided to murder them. At the last moment, however, she balked at the idea and instead transformed them into four white swans and placed the following curse on them: 'They will spend 300 years on Lake Derryvaragh, 300 on the Sea of Moyle [between Ireland and Scotland] and 300 on the Atlantic by Erris and Inishglora.' Despite their transformation the children still had human speech and sang wonderful music; people came from far and wide to talk to them and to be entranced by the beautiful sounds they made. After centuries of hardship on the freezing waters of Moyle and the Atlantic, they came to Erris, where they were cared for by a hermit and sang the music of Christian services. However, a Connacht chieftain stole them as a present for his bride, and in the princess's presence a terrible transformation befell them. Their beautiful plumage dropped off, leaving them as four white-haired, withered, miserable beings, shrunken in the decrepitude of their vast age. Then Fionnuala requested 'Lay us in one grave and place Conn on my right hand and Fiachra at my left and Hugh before my face, for there they were wont to be when I sheltered them for many a winter's night upon the seas of Moyle.' So it was done.

Despite the wind, the lack of trees and the desolate bogland, the north-west Mayo coast has a dramatic beauty, its great cliffs – often gnawed by the waves into gigantic caverns and grotesque rock formations – rising to the great buttress of Benwee Head, whose massive precipices top 820 feet. About half a mile off the coast are the truly spectacular Stags of Broad Haven, a series of seven great rocks rising out of the sea, each more than 300 feet high.

In places the bogland covers the entire landscape, extending in an unbroken sweep from cliff edges to mountain summits, averaging a depth of five feet. This blanket bog, it seems, began to grow five thousand years ago, enveloping tombs dating from 4000 BC. Some of these, as well as dry-stone walls of the same period, similar to those raised in western Ireland today, have been uncovered. Recent archaeological

Benwee Head, Co. Mayo. In the background are the Stags of Broad Haven, seven enormous rocks two miles offshore and 300 ft high.

excavations have revealed the most extensive megalithic remains in the world, and the greatest dig has been carried out at Ceide (kay-jeh) Fields, five miles west of Ballycastle, where 2500 acres have been mapped. Of course, Irish bogs often reveal treasure – hoards of gold and silver, platters, goblets, spades and spoons, and even a firkin of butter, almost three hundred years old but still edible. The largest dug-out canoe in Europe was discovered in a Galway bog.

The town of Killala is so small that you are through it before you notice it. Its bay, however, is spectacular, and probably never looked more so than when three French warships flying British colours anchored here on 22 August 1798; a French soldier landed to climb to the top of the Protestant Bishop's Palace and replace the British flag with a green flag bearing a harp and the words 'Erin go brágh' (Ireland for ever). The fact that the French found themselves welcomed by the Irish peasantry in the name of the Virgin Mary instead of the slogan of the Revolution rather startled them, and did nothing to further their joint purpose. Nonetheless, this gesture was the Directory's answer to Wolfe Tone's years of pleading in Paris for help in mounting their great rebellion. It came too late: the rebellion had been crushed already. By the time the French and their ragged band of Irish auxiliaries had reached Ballinmuck in Co. Longford their numbers had been seriously depleted and their ammunition almost all used up. Confronted by generals Cornwallis and Lake, they were easily defeated.

A month later Tone himself arrived in Lough Swilly, Co. Donegal, with a second French force, but this time the British were prepared and forced them to surrender. Tone was taken ashore and, despite his insistence that as a French officer in uniform he should be honourably shot, he was sentenced to be hanged. Rather than endure this indignity, Tone cut his throat with a penknife and endured seven agonizing days before dying.

Ballina, though Mayo's largest town, is really worth stopping at only to eat, the nearby River Moy providing succulent fresh salmon. A digression southwards will take you to Lough Conn, but you may prefer to continue along the coast, crossing the border shortly after Ballina into magical Co. Sligo. Your introduction to it is the dark blue range of the Ox Mountains, whose situation lends them great drama. It is worth stopping briefly at Inishcrone to admire the view: to your left is the great sweep of Killala Bay; to your right, the beautiful Ox range. Two miles north of the village is the ruined castle of the MacFirbis family of poets and annalists. Duald MacFirbis (1585–1670) was the last of the hereditary genealogists of Ireland. He compiled the Book of Genealogies (now in University College Library, Dublin) and Chronicon Scotorum, a history of the Irish. Both the Great Book of Lecan (now in the Royal Irish Academy) and the Yellow Book of Lecan (Trinity College) were compiled here.

One of the principal glories of Sligo is its coastline, a succession of superb beaches stretching from the white opalescent sands of Inishcrone to the vivid yellow of Mullaghmore, which faces north over Donegal Bay. Inland are the spreading well-watered plains of Tubbercurry and Ballymote, which run south and west until halted by the Bricklieve Mountains and, on the horizon, the Curlew range where, in 1599, the great Red Hugh O'Donnell routed an army led by the Governor of Connacht. West of Sligo town rises Knocknarea, an enormous truncated cone of limestone, and to the north is the Dartry range, encompassing the extraordinary flat-topped Benbulben, under whose shadow Yeats, one of the greatest English-language poets of the twentieth century, lies buried. Sligo is a land not only of myth, poetry and magnificent scenery, however, but also of history: you will find almost every phase of Irish history represented in the county, with megalithic remains as old as Newgrange.

Although larger and, as 'the gateway to the northwest', more important than Westport, Sligo town is neither so gracious nor so picturesque. I recall it years

Sligo Abbey, a Dominican friary built in 1253, and heavily restored in the fifteenth century. Its many fine memorials include one to O'Connor Sligo and his wife.

ago as a sleepy, typically indolent west of Ireland town but today, like everywhere else, it is choked with traffic. It does, however, have excellent pubs and warm-hearted inhabitants. The ruined Dominican Friary, dating from 1253, is worth a visit; most of the walls still stand and the chancel and high altar have been well preserved. And it would be a mistake not to see the Municipal Art Gallery in Stephen Street, which has a good collection of Irish work by such artists as John Yeats (father of the poet), Jack B. Yeats, Paul Henry, Evie Hone and others.

Both Rosses Point and Strandhill (noted for its Atlantic breakers) are popular resorts, with the usual fine beaches and a championship golf course. The former is also the home of the Sligo Yacht Club where many national and international championships are held. Near Strandhill is Killaspugbrone, where St Patrick lost a tooth now kept in an elaborate shrine in the National Museum in Dublin.

Knocknarea is worth climbing if only for the panorama stretching from Slieve League in Donegal to the north to Croagh Patrick in Mayo to the south, and spanning Sligo Bay, the Ox Mountains and the lakes and hills beyond Lough Gill. One of the strangest features of Knocknarea, however, is 'Maeve's Mound', a great grey cairn of stones which crowns the summit. Measuring some 200 feet across and over 35 feet high, it is estimated to weigh forty thousand tons, and under it the queen-goddess is said to be buried. From Knocknarea it is relatively easy to reach Carrowmore Megalithic Cemetery; apart from Carnac in Brittany, this is the largest concentration of Bronze Age chambered tombs in Europe, extending over a mile and a half of undulating countryside. With their mushroom-shaped capstones and enormous boulders blocking their entrances, they are an awesome sight. Not so long ago there were more than a hundred and fifty cairns

The arduous climb to the Carrowkeel Bronze Age cemetery in the Bricklieve Mountains, Sligo, is rewarded with marvellous panoramas like this one.

here, all marking the sites of tombs, but over the years they have been despoiled by local farmers so that today that figure has been considerably reduced.

Near Knocknarea, too, is a beauty spot called The Glen, where a tremendous natural chasm, about a mile long and with sheer 50-foot cliffs on either side, has been created in the limestone. It appears at first to be choked with trees and vegetation, particularly ferns, but a track of sorts leads through a series of enchanted glades that are among the most picturesque in Ireland.

The country to the south of Sligo town is well worth exploring, especially around Ballymote. From the Fairy Mound of Laughter, a tumulus thickly carpeted with daisies in summer, there are wonderful views. About a mile to the east of the head of Lough Arrow is 'The Labby' or Carrickglass Portal Grave, one of the most eccentric-looking objects you are ever likely to see. It has a weathered capstone 8 feet thick, 15 feet long and 9 feet wide which has been estimated to weight 70 tons, but what makes it so extraordinary is that it sports a great wig of heather on top which at first sight makes it look like a drunken judge. Just beyond this rakish monument lies Lough Nasool, which is reputed to disappear completely on occasion – it last vanished in 1964 – but it always returns.

Magnificent Lough Arrow, with its azure blue waters and ringlets of miniature islands, and the Bricklieve Mountains, just six miles to the south of Ballymote, should not be missed. The Bricklieves consist of five parallel limestone ridges separated by deep canyons; above these gashes are innumerable prehistoric cairns, some more than 20 feet high, surrounded as at Newgrange by enormous boulder kerbstones. This is Carrowkeel Cemetery. The eastern-most ridge above Lough Arrow is the most fantastical: there the cairns ascend in a series of terraces, each separated from the others by steep cliffs; on the second is the area known as 'The Village', consisting of some fifty rings of stones, many of them fronted by standing pillars. Ideally you need to allow a full day to explore the Bricklieves, tramping through their purple heather and, in particular, drinking in the superb sunrises and sunsets to be seen from the top.

159

Just three miles to the south of Ballymote are the Caves of Keshcorran, where a whole series of cave entrances can be seen some 600 feet up in the limestone cliffs. The bones of pre-Ice Age animals – elk, reindeer, bear and Arctic lemming – have been found in these caves as well as traces of ancient human habitation. Cormac MacAirt, third-century king of Tara – who coordinated and regularized the laws of Ireland, introduced the windmill and carried out successful raids on Britain – was born in one of these caves and suckled, it is claimed, by a she-wolf.

Ballymote itself grew up around a fourteenth-century castle built by Richard de Burgo. It changed hands many times, however, and is now best remembered by the Irish themselves as the place from which Red Hugh O'Donnell started out on his fateful march to the terrible defeat at Kinsale. The greatest of Irish codices, the Book of Ballymote (now in the Royal Irish Academy) was written in the local Franciscan Friary, among its contents being the highly controversial Book of Invasions. This is the manuscript that gives the key to the system of linear or runic writing known as ogham, which was based on the Roman alphabet and was extensively used in Ireland and Celtic areas of Britain in the fourth and fifth centuries. The Ballymote area is also famous for its traditional music.

I must warn you that not all Sligo is bewitching scenery and romantic views. The area near Sligo town is the antithesis of what many visitors would like Ireland to be: caravans infest the coastline and tourist coaches back up amid the sand dunes. As Ireland becomes as consumer mad as the rest of the western world, the motor car pervades one scenic gem after another, modern bungalows of an almost depraved incongruity mushroom everywhere, and this wild and beautiful country is being systematically turned into a vast suburbia. House prices around Sligo Bay have risen steeply, mainly due to an influx of continentals; now there are so many foreigners, particularly Germans, living on Raghly Peninsula that the area has been dubbed 'Little Bavaria'.

East of Sligo town, however, opening out from the pleasant Garavogue River, is Lough Gill, a place of great natural beauty and the setting for Yeats's famous poem 'The Lake Isle of Innisfree'. Woodland covers the gentle hills that rise from the banks of the lake, and the vegetation on the many islets includes arbutus, whitebeam and yew, with ground cover of many rare plants and flowers. In its quiet, uncontaminated beauty it is a welcome reminder of what Ireland has always been. Among the places of interest nearby is the highly restored Parkes Castle, originally dating from the seventeenth century, which is sited picturesquely on the lough's eastern shore, and not far away are the ruins of Dromahair Castle, from which Dervorgilla eloped with Dermot MacMurrough while her husband was on a pilgrimage to Lough Derg.

A short diversion from Sligo will take you north to Glencar, a beautiful lake where steep-sided mountains rising to 2000 feet surround a glacial valley. The lake is fed by the Differeen River and flows out into the Drumcliff River, which then drops a sheer fifty feet in a spectacular cascade. The whole area, indeed, is a mass of waterfalls, cascading down the sides of the mountains. One called 'The Stream in the Face of the Height' looks a bit startling when the wind reaches a certain strength and the water appears to flow upwards.

Yeats is buried in Drumcliff churchyard. The site is, unfortunately, no longer as romantic as when he was alive, for main road traffic roars past only a few yards away, running, in fact, through the old monastic site founded by Columcille; there the remains of a round tower and a tenth-century high cross still stand, looking oddly out of place amid all the uproar. Still, once inside the churchyard itself, the beauty of the place becomes apparent. Inland, to the north and east, are Benbulben and the King's Mountain – Benbulben, magical as ever, changing colour and contour as you view it from different angles. Its truncated top ends in a great bluff, almost like the overflow on a pint of

---

A romantic corner of Lough Gill, Co. Sligo. The lake was made famous by W. B. Yeats's poem, 'The Lake Isle of Innisfree'.

Guinness, and then falls in a steeply inclined concave cliff some 1600 feet high.

I have already referred to Dermot's death fight with the Enchanted Boar on these very slopes (see p. 18). To conclude the story, when the boar charged, Dermot fell across its back and was carried some distance before he was thrown to the ground; then the beast sprang upon him, 'ripping out his bowels'. Simultaneously Dermot used the hilt of his sword to dash out its brains and it fell dead beside him. While Dermot writhed in agony, Finn approached and began taunting him, 'Would that all the women in Ireland could see thee now; for thy excellent beauty is turned to ugliness'. Dermot reminded him that he had once saved him from death and begged him to heal him, for Finn had the magic gift of restoring the wounded with well-water. By the time Finn had given in to the entreaties of other members of the Fianna and brought him water, Dermot was dead.

The story of Dermot and Grania and their sixteen-year flight round Ireland pursued by the vengeful Finn is, of course, one of ancient Ireland's great love stories, and the irony of the tale is maintained to the very end. Years after Dermot's death, Finn, judging that the lapse of time is bound to have softened Grania's attitude towards him, approaches her. At first she treats him with scorn and indignation but he woos her with such tenderness that at last she succumbs, and he brings her back as his bride to his fortress on the Hill of Allen.

I remember a London journalist friend of mine returning years ago from an assignment to Co. Donegal and declaring, 'it is the poorest land I have ever seen.' It is true that much of Donegal is covered by blanket bog and is virtually unenclosed, uninhabited and treeless. Its northern rocks, the oldest in Ireland, consist of an agglomeration of rugged gneisses and schists, with granite, marble and more gneiss among

The remarkable craggy slopes of Benbulben, Co. Sligo. Here the great champion Finn MacCool exacted revenge on Dermot, who had eloped with his intended bride.

even older rocks inland. Eroded by extensive glaciation in prehistoric times, it has been lashed and torn by the Atlantic and high winds for millennia (even today, thatch on cottage roofs has to be tied down vertically and horizontally, and the ends of the ropes pegged to the walls or weighed down by small boulders to keep it from flying away). Yet the truth is that its wild and craggy undulations, its awesome mountainous scarps, myriad rivers, lakes and waterfalls, and its spectacular 200-mile coastline make it one of the most beautiful regions of Ireland.

It is a place of paradoxes and mysteries. Wild and windy it may be, yet its climate is as mild as Kerry's. There are unusual natural phenomena, such as raised beaches left high and dry when the ice receded, and religious enigmas such as a strong devotion to St Catherine, whose remains still rest in a Coptic monastery, and Greek crosses incised in ancient grave slabs. There is evidence that the Donegal coast was first inhabited seven thousand years ago, but today the second largest of all Irish counties is one of the least populated. Though not easily accessible, it attracts thousands of visitors every summer, yet the influx has done nothing to diminish the numbers of Irish-speakers. Ireland's most northerly county, it is part of Ulster, yet it is also part of southern Ireland (the Republic). Neither of the two great monastic foundations established by its greatest son, Columcille ('Dove of the Church'), lies within its borders – one is at Derry and the other on Iona, in Scotland. It is a land full of garrulous 'shannackies' (storytellers) who talk about the great saint as though he is still alive today, and regale you with interminable but entertaining tales of how they met the Blessed Virgin, yet it still boasts an enclave of the most taciturn people in Ireland. And it is a county where fact is often hard to separate from fiction. The people of Ballyshannon, in the south-western corner, claim to be descendants of the first inhabitants of Ireland. Donegal town claims to be over two thousand years old, making it the oldest urban centre still flourishing. On the shores of Lough Akibborn is a small church called the Oratory of Columcille, and beside it lies the Natal Stone on which

the saint was born; even today pregnant women come to lie on it to ensure an easy delivery. There is scarcely a cottage in the south-west of the county where you will not hear 'true' stories of fairies stealing human beings, of banshees warning of death and witches casting spells, of mermaids loving human beings and of men and women 'with the Evil Eye'.

For sheer beauty, I advise you to stick to the coastline as far as possible, though a few diversions, such as a visit to Lough Derg, even if you are not a believer, are well worth while. Lough Derg, one of the world's most famous places of pilgrimage, lies in the far south of the county. The original shrine, St Patrick's Purgatory', was probably on a little island called Saint's Island to which pilgrims from all over Europe came in medieval times – from Santiago de Compostela itself and even from Hungary. In 1479 Sixtus IV ordered an inquiry into its authenticity, and eighteen years later the infamous Borgia Pope, Alexander VI, ordered that it be destroyed. Yet pilgrims continued to come, and it was not until 1632, on the orders of the local Protestant bishop, that the Augustinian Priory which had replaced Patrick's original foundation was destroyed. At some indeterminate date the pilgrimage shrine was moved to Station Island, where a huge octagonal neo-romanesque church stands today. For devout Irish Catholics a visit to Lough Derg falls almost into the same category as a visit to Mecca for Muslims.

The first of Donegal's great beaches as you drive up from the south is Rossnowlagh ('the beautiful cove'), more then three miles of perfect sand running along the east coast of Donegal Bay. Donegal town, on the River Eske, is worth stopping at just to see its castle; a ruined Jacobean structure, now being restored, it incorporated the remains of the old headquarters of the O'Donnells. Red Hugh himself had destroyed the original fortified tower-house so that it could not be

Station Island, Lough Derg, Co. Donegal. St Patrick's shrine here has been one of the great European places of Christian pilgrimage since the early Middle Ages.

used by the English; however, the eventual grantee of the property was a Sir Basil Brooke who acquired it in 1623 after 'The Flight of the Earls' (when O'Neill and Red Hugh's successor, and more than ninety other leading Gaels of Ulster, fled Ireland for ever). Beautifully situated on the Eske, too, are the ruins of Donegal Abbey, a Franciscan foundation where the Annals of the Four Masters were written. This was a history of the Irish compiled by four of the monks from all known documents, starting in 2958 BC and ending in AD 1616. The authenticity of many of these early documents might be gauged from the fact that the first entry is dated forty years before the Flood and refers to a visit to Ireland by Noah's granddaughter.

From Donegal town you may be tempted to explore the softer countryside around Lough Eske, with its stunning background of the Blue Stack Mountains. But the spectacular coastal route leads west via Killybegs, one of the centres of the Donegal carpet and tweed making industry, to Carrick, where a local pub boasts the largest selection of whiskies – Irish, Scotch, Bourbon, Lowland and Highland malts, even a Chinese variety – you are likely to encounter anywhere. To the west lies the inviting scenery of Teelin Bay, whose hinterland of rapids and pools offers fine fishing. Slieve League (1972 feet) is the highest mountain in the area, and a frontal attack up One Man's Path, a vertiginous sea-cliff track only two feet wide, is a challenging climb for any amateur. Make your way first to Bunglass Point, and continue to Amharc Mor (The Great View), from which you can admire the great cliffs towering above you, stained with brightly coloured minerals. Here you face a steep climb of 1024 feet. One Man's Path is a knife-edged ridge with an 1800-foot sheer drop to the ocean on one side and a precipice falling to an inland lough on the other.

The road from Carrick to Glen Bay runs through desolate, heather-covered moorland so that it is almost a relief to reach the verdant glen of Glencolumbkille, a place of pilgrimage since the seventh century. Saint Columcille himself founded a monastery here, of which fifteen pillars decorated with crosses and geometrical designs are all that is left. He then chased all the demons and venomous reptiles that had somehow eluded Patrick on his mountain out of Ireland for good. Every year, on 15 June, there is a three-mile pilgrimage around the site, starting at midnight and ending with Mass at three o'clock in the morning.

The glen has been inhabited for six thousand years (the whole area is rich in cairns and dolmens) but by the first half of this century the population had died away almost to nothing. Then in 1952 a priest called Father James McDyer came to the village. He found that eighty per cent of the young people were being forced to emigrate through lack of employment and set about providing both work and facilities for them. Within a few years he had opened a community hall, had electricity installed in the glen, had new roads laid, water piped in, a holiday village set up, four factories started and a folk museum established. Emigration was dramatically halted and the people found a new pride in themselves.

You leave the glen by way of dramatic Glengesh Pass (The Glen of the Swans) which winds down through the mountains towards Ardara in twisting, alpine style. It is worth diverging just before the town and making for Maghera, where the lake scenery, steep mountainsides and Essaranka Waterfall are a magnificent sight. From Ardara itself make for Glenties, a 'planter's town' (referring to the Plantation of Ulster in 1610) which aspires to some elegance, and thence to stunning Gweebarra Bay. A short detour here takes you round Crohy Head, where you find yourself hemmed in on one side by mountains and on the other by rocks and pinnacles against which the sea dashes with such fury that they seem permanently wrapped in great plumes of water and spray. From here you are quickly into the Rosses (promontories), regarded by many Irish as 'the real Ireland' (the district is entirely Irish-speaking), a rugged, stony-soiled sixty thousand acres stretching northwards from Dunglow to Crolly. It is a windswept region of humpy heatherland inlaid with a hundred and twenty lakes and tiny, well-worked fields. The main coast road to Gweedore from Burtonport (which claims to land more salmon and lobster than any other port in Ireland) passes through a landscape of heavy boulders and fissured rocks.

You now have the option of continuing round the coast to Bloody Foreland (so-called because of the brilliance of its sunsets) or making for the central area of north Donegal which loses nothing in comparison with the coastline. The inland road runs along the northern shores of loughs Nacung and Dunlewy, giving you your first proper sight of Mount Errigal (2466 feet), a magnificent quartzite cone which rises in solitary grandeur above the other peaks of the Derryveagh range. From its summit, if you wish to exert yourself, you can see a vast panorama extending from the mountains of western Scotland to the Twelve Bens of Connemara. Even if you choose not to climb, the country between Errigal and Lough Gartan, to the south-east, should really be walked. This is the Glenveagh National Park, a wonderland of hills and gorges where red deer run wild. It is watered by the serpentine Glenveagh River, which empties into Lough Beagh, and by beautiful cascades like long plumes which drop down sheer cliff sides into valleys filled with rhododendron and tall spruce.

It is worth making the difficult drive to Lough Gartan, partly for the exquisite scenery and partly because it was here that Columcille himself was born. A colossal cross marks the spot. Nearby is a Bronze Age slab where the saint used to sleep; it is known as the Flagstone of Loneliness because people about to emigrate used to come here to pray the night before their departure in the hope of being protected from homesickness. A few miles to the north is the Rock of Doon where for two thousand years O'Donnell chieftains were crowned with great ceremony.

You cannot hope to see all the wonders of Donegal in one visit but do not ignore Horn Head. It stands at the tip of its own peninsula, at the entrance to Sheephaven Bay, and is among the finest headlands in the whole

Gweebarra Bay, Co. Donegal. Great scything bays and estuaries such as this are a feature of this wild, often barren, but beautiful county.

country; a giant rock over 600 feet high with ledges zigzagging down to the water, it is a great perching place for all sorts of sea-birds. A short distance to the south lies Creeslough, opposite Muckish Mountain and Doe Castle, which was the headquarters of the MacSweeneys from the early fifteenth century until roughly a hundred years ago. They had come to Ireland from Scotland as gallowglasses and did much to stiffen native resistance to the English. The great Red Hugh learned his military skills here as a boy.

Rathmullan, on the western shore of Lough Swilly, occupies a special niche in Irish history. It was from here that the boy Red Hugh was kidnapped in 1587 and incarcerated for many years in Dublin Castle. This was also the scene of The Flight of the Earls, that momentous episode in 1609 when Gaelic Ireland was finally extinguished.

On the far side of Lough Swilly is the great Inishowen peninsula, probably the least visited and least known part of Donegal, although its scenery equals the best in the county. Its northernmost tip is Malin Head, Ireland's John O'Groats, and its main town is Buncrana, now a bustling seaside resort, where Wolfe Tone was taken ashore after his capture aboard a French warship. Its most spectacular feature, however, is the Grìanán of Aileach, a great circular stone enclosure with dry-stone walls 17 feet high and 17 feet thick, standing 803 feet up on the bare side of Greenan Mountain. Once this was the royal palace and meeting place of the O'Neills, rulers of Tír-Eoghain (pronounced Teer-owen and anglicized as Tyrone), a strange, brooding place nowadays surrounded by evidence of earlier Bronze Age settlements. Isolated and lonely on its windswept hill, it offers superb views along both Lough Swilly and Lough Foyle towards the sea.

These are the waters Columcille sailed on his journey to Iona, and these are the verses he is said to have written to describe the event:

> Too swiftly my coracle flies on her way
> From Derry I mournfully turned the prow;
> I grieve at the errand which drives me today
> To the land of the Ravens, to Alba, now.
>
> How swiftly we glide! there is a grey eye
> Looks back upon Erin, but it no more
> Shall see while the stars shall endure in the sky
> Her women, her men, or her stainless shore.

Mount Errigal, Co. Donegal, is the north-west's highest peak at 2468 ft. A brilliant quartzite cone, it glistens like silver when the mists clear and the sun shines.

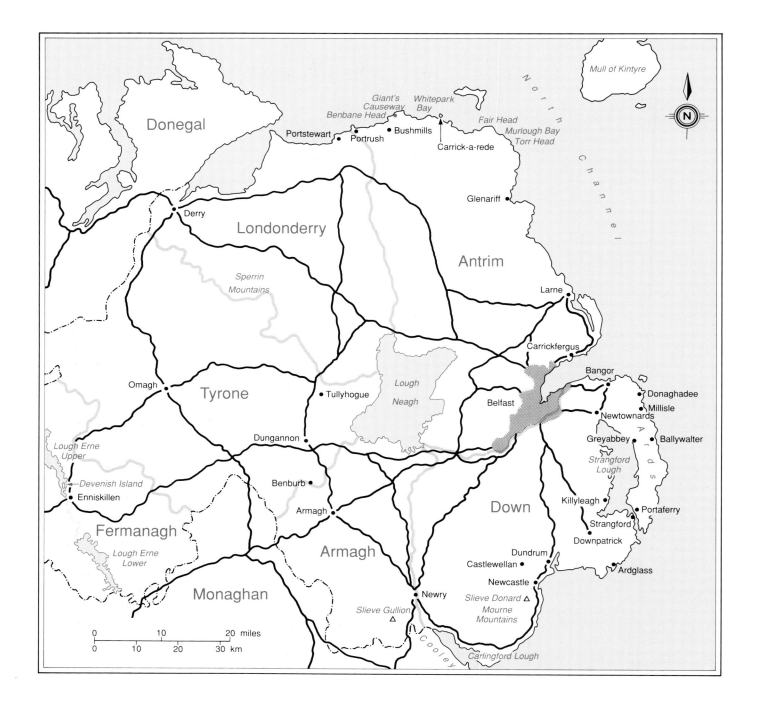

6
Belfast and the North

Carrickfergus – Glens of Antrim – Giant's Causeway – Derry
Fermanagh Lakelands – Armagh – The Mournes
Strangford Lough – Bangor

The province of Northern Ireland consists of six of Ulster's nine counties, comprising an area of 5500 square miles. It is roughly 110 miles wide and 85 from top to bottom, with the great expanse of Lough Neagh (covering 153 square miles, it is the largest lake in the British Isles) roughly in its centre. It is, of course, part of the United Kingdom. Its capital, Belfast, is the very essence of the North, capital of a different Ireland: a city rich in paradox, crippled by much industrial nastiness yet set amid considerable beauty. Few capitals in the world enjoy such a magnificent position.

A red-brick city built from the Triassic sandstone of the Lagan Valley, it sits at the head of a twelve-mile-long sea lough which opens out on to the North Channel and the Atlantic. From hills around it, the panoramas are spectacular, especially, on a clear day, towards the east, where great tracts of Western Scotland and its islands extend across the horizon, clad in Cezanne blue. The eastern side of Belfast Lough is the quiet side, where neat, undulating countryside, rising no more than 600 feet, slides away to the beaches of the small Co. Down resorts which make up many of the city's dormitories. Spacious houses line the shore, backed by thickly wooded slopes of ash, beech and

sycamore, while flotillas of yachts and dinghies bob contentedly at anchor. The west side is much the more dramatic of the two, its irregular hills, which create a great rampart to the west of the city, bobbing down the lough like the humps of sea monsters, past Kilroot where Swift enjoyed his first living and wrote *Tale of a Tub*, to end in the dramatic cliffs of Black Head.

This backdrop of green hills, terminating in the cleft rock known as Cave Hill, gives even the most desolate of the city's back streets a heart-lifting prospect. At nightfall, after sunsets that are often as spectacular as those of Africa or California, yellow sodium street lights colour the sky and reflect in the shimmering lough as if the city were decked out for Mardi Gras. At times like these it is hard to believe that behind the glittering façade Belfast festers with lethal and anachronistic bitterness.

It is a place of verve and vitality, a city with tang. Despite its deplorable history of sectarian strife, it is a warm-hearted town. Its people are gregarious, ready for 'crack' or a yarn at the slightest excuse, although heavily imbued with the Protestant work ethic. The capital of a Bible belt, it seems more religion-ridden than anywhere else in Ireland, yet few Protestants actually attend church regularly. All social life is coloured by whether you are 'Prod' (most Irish people pronounce Protestant as 'Proddestant') or Fenian (Catholic), biblical tags confront you everywhere and the city is awash with home-made evangelists bellowing that they have been 'saved'. Accents, which derive from places as disparate as Devon, the Scottish Borders, Galloway and Glasgow, may sound rough but manners are uniformly good. In spite of decades of civil conflict, most Belfast people boast of their quality of life though this admittedly reflects not so much the grandeur of their city as the ease with which they can get out of it and into the countryside beyond. Quite literally within minutes of the City Hall, you can bathe in the sea, climb a mountain, shoot game, fish in the open sea or in silent, reed-bounded lakes, go yachting, play golf (there are eight courses around the city), inspect Norman castles or classical mansions, wander in superb forest parks and explore glens which echo with the sound of plashing waterfalls, or simply drive along almost empty roads through breathtaking scenery. Best of all, there is no overcrowding and the sheer tempo of life is agreeable.

Belfast has enjoyed a remarkable rise. In 1688 a hundred and fifty houses clustered round a castle built by Sir Arthur Chichester, Lord Deputy of Ireland and chief beneficiary of the Plantation of Ulster, which saw the native Irish largely displaced by English and Scots. Carrickfergus, eleven miles further down the lough – where in the twelfth century the Normans had built a castle (still intact) – was Ulster's principal town. By this time the language of Belfast had become English, spoken with a strong Devonian burr. The arrival of Louis Crommelin from Picardy, whom William III had appointed Linen Overseer of Ireland, had a dynamic effect on its development. He introduced French Huguenots, along with new Dutch machinery and methods, transforming linen manufacturing in the Lagan Valley and turning Belfast into its main marketplace. Then, with the foundation of Harland & Wolff in 1859 (for decades the largest shipyard in the world and still one of the largest), Belfast abruptly found itself the industrial capital of Ireland. Population soared as impoverished Scots flooded in; from twenty thousand in 1800, its population had grown to three hundred and eighty-seven thousand by 1911 and half a million by the outbreak of World War II.

For most of the eighteenth century Belfast men had held sternly radical views; indeed, the Society of United Irishmen, forerunner of today's Republican Movement, had been founded in Belfast – and by Protestants at that. However, rapid growth, the obvious benefits of union with Britain and a fresh influx of Scots wedded to an extreme form of Calvinism quickly turned Belfast into a zealously intolerant Protestant city. The attempt by native Catholics to obtain a share of the new wealth produced major sectarian riots. There were no fewer than fifteen major outbreaks between 1813 and 1914, some almost verging on civil war. There was sustained trouble in 1919–21, another outbreak in 1935, yet another in 1964 and a series of disturbances beginning in 1969 which continue to this day.

There is a temptation to leave Belfast to hone its nose on the grindstones of industry and sectarianism, and to ignore its importance in other fields. But this would be unfair. In the eighteenth century it was a city of poets and scholars, and in the nineteenth it saw the births of the poet Sir Samuel Ferguson, the scientist Lord Kelvin, the painter Sir John Lavery, the novelist Forrest Reid and the dramatist St John Ervine. During the first half of this century it produced only one notable poet, Louis MacNeice (with John Hewitt adding a minor key) but since World War II it can claim an outstanding novelist in Brian Moore and a clutch of respectable poets such as Derek Mahon, Roy McFadden and Michael Longley. Musically, Belfast has produced at least one world-class instrumentalist in the flautist James Galway, and the Ulster Orchestra is probably Ireland's best. For all its seemingly ineradicable defects, then, it is not a cultural desert.

Though architecturally graceless, Belfast's city hall, with its massive neo-baroque frontages, still reflects the high confidence and optimism of the Edwardian city.

The Crown Liquor Saloon, Belfast, is one of the surviving great Victorian gin palaces. John Betjeman called it 'the many-coloured cavern'.

Modern Belfast has only one or two high-rise buildings and is dominated by two giant shipyard cranes, Samson and Goliath, which loom heavily out of scale with the rest of the city. Its grandest building is the City Hall, completed in 1906 by Sir Thomas Brumwell, who had to sue the Corporation for his fees. For sheer size and spaciousness of setting, there is probably no more impressive civic headquarters in the British Isles; indeed, one would have to travel far to find its equal. Built of white Portland stone, it has a main façade some 300 feet long, a dome 173 feet high and an interior, rich with Italian marble, as sumptuous as a Roman palace (one of its most spectacular rooms is an oak-panelled banqueting hall destroyed in the 1941 Blitz, which was rebuilt in 1953). Yet the City Hall has rightly been described as 'architecturally boorish'

and, for all its baroque presumptions, it is not a graceful building.

Donegall Square, in which this monster stands, is a bright and airy place and a repository of Victoriana. Indeed, before World War II Belfast itself could be said to have been pickled in Victorian aspic; it had some half-dozen stupendous nineteenth-century department stores of which the Bank Buildings, with its Italianate façade, and Robinson & Cleaver, a six-storeyed affair topped with slender cupolas – where Queen Victoria and the Maharajah of Cooch Behar bought their linen – were outstanding. Aside from the City Hall, Donegall Square itself has two buildings of which any city might feel proud, the massive Scottish Provident building on the west side, with its extraordinary array of stone sculptures – queens, dolphins, lions' heads, sphinxes – and a warehouse constructed like a Venetian palazzo.

Central Belfast can be walked in the course of an hour or so. Near the docks are the Albert Memorial Clock (the Big Ben of Belfast) and a fine Custom House designed by Charles Lanyon who was responsible for some of the city's most distinguished buildings. Nearby Waring Street boasts Lanyon's Belfast Banking Company (the oldest in the city), built in the eighteenth century as Assembly Rooms, and the Ulster Bank, an overpowering Italianate building of yellow sandstone with fluted pillars and intricately designed iron railings. Your next stop might be St Anne's Cathedral, a neo-romanesque Church of Ireland building interesting because it is the last resting place of Lord Carson, the Dublin lawyer who led Ulster resistance to Home Rule in the early part of this century. To the west of this lies Clifton House, one of the best buildings in the city; a fine Georgian-style charitable institution of 1771–4, it boasts an unusual octagonal-based stone spire.

Retracing your steps to the city centre, look for Great Victoria Street, which begins with two notable buildings – the Royal Belfast Academical Institution ('Inst'), a classical eighteenth-century building designed by Sir John Soane, and the College of Technology, an Edwardian essay in Portland stone which, like the

City Hall, is imposing if nothing else. A few hundred yards along is the Grand Opera House, designed by Frank Matcham, where a dull exterior gives way to a riotous Victorian extravaganza inside, all gilded boxes and elephant buttresses. Almost opposite is the Crown Liquor Saloon, a National Trust property and a must for every visitor. The exterior is a medley of coloured tiles – yellow, green, blue, amber, carmine – while the interior has fine Victorian stucco work, a scrolled ceiling, highly decorated woodwork and a range of closed 'snugs' where small parties can foregather in private. The rest of Great Victoria Street has now become known as the Golden Mile because of the number of restaurants – French, Italian, Greek, Chinese and Indian – which have opened in the past decade. Although there is ample variety, I cannot pretend that anything like *haute cuisine* is on offer.

Queen's University, designed by Lanyon, is red-brick mock Tudor and dates from 1849. It is approached by fine Georgian terraces – Upper and Lower Crescent are worth looking at – and University Square, flanking the university, has the best-preserved row of Georgian houses in the city. At right angles to this row is the Theological College, an Italianate design, again by Lanyon, which was the headquarters of the Northern Ireland Parliament until 1932. Some hundred yards or so to the south lie the Botanic Gardens, a superb little park which houses Lanyon's famous Palm House; older than Kew's although similar in design, it was in fact the first glasshouse in the world. Nearby is the Ulster Museum which houses treasures from the *Girona*, the Armada ship wrecked off Co. Antrim. The Museum has exhaustive collections covering an astonishing range of subjects, and several good art galleries.

In a city of churches three are worth particular mention: the pretty little First Presbyterian church in Rosemary Street, which delighted John Wesley; St George's in High Street, which has a splendid classical façade, and St Malachy's Catholic church in Alfred Street, which has a magnificent fan-vaulted ceiling.

Stormont – visible from wherever you go in the city – is worth a closer look; a huge neo-classical gift from Britain, it housed Northern Ireland's Parliament

The Palm House, Belfast Botanic Gardens. Built in 1834, it is the oldest hothouse in the world, pre-dating the one at Kew in London by ten years.

for many years. To the north of the city, on the slopes of Cave Hill, are Bellevue and Hazelwood parks which house the zoo. If you have the energy you should scramble up to McArt's Fort on the top of Cave Hill, where Wolfe Tone, Henry Joy McCracken and other United Irishmen plotted rebellion in 1795 and, Protestants all, pledged themselves to the cause of Irish independence.

Leaving the capital behind you, head north along Belfast Lough to Carrickfergus, from whose castle walls Ulstermen witnessed the United States' first naval victory, when in April 1778 John Paul Jones shrugged aside the menace of the castle's guns and captured the British warship *Drake*. St Nicholas's parish church, contemporaneous with the castle, contains a monument to Sir Arthur Chichester

(1563–1625), a grandiose kneeling group in marble and alabaster. The parents of the United States president Andrew Jackson emigrated from Carrickfergus in 1765 and a small museum of his memorabilia has been erected here.

If you see little else in the North, I do recommend that you take the Antrim Coast Road (sometimes compared to the Mediterranean corniche but really quite different in character), a sixty-mile drive that will lead you past the superb Glens of Antrim to one of the world's wonders, The Giant's Causeway. Once past Larne, the scenery is ravishing. To your left looms Slemish (1437 feet), the mountain where Patrick is said to have tended sheep as a slave after he had been seized from his home in Britain (though modern scholarship tends to place his captivity in Mayo). To your right lies the glorious Sea of Moyle, now prosaically named the North Channel, on which the Children of Lir were buffeted for 300 years. The road bends and twists around majestic bays with mighty headlands jutting out as far as the eye can see; here the Scottish coast is so close that the Mull of Kintyre, only thirteen miles away, seems like just another Irish headland. As you travel north you pass through sleepy little fishing villages lying at the foot of the Glens. Running inland for some miles, the Glens are an unspoiled region of rushing streams and rivers, cascading waterfalls and tall hedges of blackthorn, hawthorn and ash, lit in spring and summer by yellow gorse, fuchsia and riotous displays of white, blue and yellow wild flowers. If you have time it is well worth exploring these glens and I particularly recommend Glenariff, whose forest park looks out over superb vistas of sea, sky and wooded landscape. The coast road, flanked by impressive rock formations, passes through corniche-style tunnels and arches, and emerges at quaint harbours and magnificent bays: Murlough and White-park (National Trust) are ideal for bathing. A steep and winding scenic route, a diversion from the main road, leads you past Torr Head to a scrubby, boggy plateau which ends at the vertiginous heights of Fair Head (626 feet high). It is worth studying the rock formations here. The molten lava that created the extraordinary configurations of the Causeway buried a series of older rocks – red standstone, blue clay, iron ore, coal and chalk among others – and the headland itself boasts sixteen different rock strata. This is a superlative vantage point for Rathlin Island, which has one pub, one guesthouse and a hundred inhabitants. If you are undaunted by the heights of Fair Head, try the rope bridge at Carrick-a-rede, further west; swaying 80 feet above the waves, it is made of planks strung between wires and it thumps up and down as soon as you set foot on it. Nor is there any safety net.

After Ballycastle, with its fine beach and championship links, press on past the road to the Causeway to visit Bushmills, the world's oldest distillery, where you are likely to be entertained to a free glass or two of one of the planet's finest products. A little further on is Dunluce Castle; perched on a great crag over the sea, it is the very epitome of romanticism; It once belonged to the Mandevilles, a French family who took the Irish-sounding name of McQuillans and held it until Sorley Boy MacDonnell captured it by a ruse. In the mid-seventeenth century Sorley Boy's descendants, the Earls of Antrim, abandoned Dunluce and allowed to to fall into picturesque decay.

The Causeway itself is a conglomerate of tightly packed basalt columns whose tops form stepping stones leading out to sea from the foot of the cliffs. Altogether, there are about forty thousand of these columns, mostly hexagonal but some with four, five, seven or eight sides. The tallest rise to 40 feet and those in the cliff face are 90 feet thick in places. To do the Causeway properly you should follow a five-mile circular walk down by the Grand Causeway and along a path which leads past awesome natural amphitheatres and strange rock formations such as the Organ, the Wishing Well and the Giant's Granny; it continues past Port na Spanaigh, where the *Girona's*

Stormont, Belfast. The building was a gift to the Northern Ireland Parliament, set up at Belfast as a result of the 1921 partition of Ireland.

treasure was recovered in 1967, and up a wooden staircase to Benbane Head and thence back along the cliff top. The ancient Irish, of course, attributed the whole thing not to the cooling effects of the sea on molten igneous rock but to the marvellous powers of Finn MacCool. Having fallen in love with a Scottish giantess who lived on the island of Staffa, he began building a road to reach her; you can see the results of his efforts on the other side too, Fingal being merely a variant of Finn. Finn's fight with a Scottish giant also created two notable landmarks – Lough Neagh and the Isle of Man: finding the going hard, Finn clawed an immense lump of land from the earth nearby and flung it at the opposing giant, but it was so heavy that it skewed out of his hand and landed in the Irish Sea.

Crossing the border from Antrim into Londonderry, you can now sample the delights of Portrush and Portstewart, agreeable enough little resorts with fine beaches. Derry (or Londonderry) is Northern Ireland's second city, and its defiance of James II helped to create British history. Columcille founded his famous monastery here before exiling himself to Iona, and the place became known as Derry Columcille. In the seventeenth century the Crown granted lands here, along with bits of Tyrone and Antrim, to the City of London who set up the Honourable Irish Society to manage them; both town and newly-carved county were then renamed Londonderry, still a matter of controversy.

The city has some fine eighteenth-century buildings and a noble Guildhall whose stained-glass windows tell the story of Derry. The seventeenth-century walls, (20–25 feet high, 30 feet wide and a mile in circumference) are still intact. There are two fine cathedrals – the Anglican St Columb's, which houses relics of the city's history, and St Eugene's Catholic Cathedral. It was at Limavady, a few miles to the east, that in 1851 Jane

Carrickfergus Castle, Co. Antrim. It was built in 1180, probably by John de Courcy, the first Norman to penetrate the Ulster fastness.

Ross listened raptly to an itinerant fiddler playing a tune which she was to make world famous – the 'Londonderry Air' (originally 'O'Cahan's Lament'); it later became popular in America as 'Danny Boy'.

Ulster is, of course, the second homeland of the people known in America as 'The Scotch-Irish'. In the eighteenth century some quarter of a million dissenters from English rule and Anglicanism fled to America, where they played a leading part in the fight for Independence. Five signed the Declaration, which was printed by John Dunlap of Strabane. At least a dozen United States presidents, including Ulysses S. Grant and Woodrow Wilson, had Ulster ancestry. Other famous Ulster emigrants included the Mellons, Rand MacNallys, Davy Crockett, Sam Houston, Mark Twain and Stephen Foster, while the first white child born west of the Rockies was Catherine O'Hara who came from the Mourne Mountains district. A Heritage Trail has been set up for Americans seeking Northern Irish ancestral roots, and an Ulster-American Folk Park has been established near Omagh in Co. Tyrone. The journey to Omagh takes you through the gentle, rather mysterious Sperrin Mountains, a rich repository of ancient monuments, to Enniskillen, 'capital' of the Fermanagh lakeland district.

Enniskillen itself is worth a brief stay. It sits on an island in the rivers connecting Upper and Lower Lough Erne. Its most spectacular sight is the Watergate, a mini-turreted affair erected by an ancestor of the Earls of Enniskillen on the site of an old Gaelic fortress; it now houses the county museum with its relics of the famous Inniskilling Regiment. Before leaving Enniskillen you may care to pay obeisance to Portora Royal School, where both Oscar Wilde and Samuel Beckett were educated. Not far from the town are two of Northern Ireland's finest mansions, Florence Court (a few miles south), former home of the earls of Enniskillen, and Castle Coole (a mile or two east), seat of the Earl of Belmore, both now owned by the National Trust. Of the two, Castle Coole, designed by James Wyatt in the 1790s and claimed to be his finest work, is the more impressive. An immense Palladian structure of Portland stone, it has a 280-foot-long façade with Doric columns and superb pavilions. The interior is classical with a glorious circular saloon.

Fermanagh is one-third water and it is the glories of the fifty-mile stretch of Upper and Lower Lough Erne that claim most of one's attention. Quiet, peaceful and set in tranquil scenery, the lakes offer exceptional fishing: several varieties of trout, including char, the trout's Ice Age predecessor, salmon, pike, roach, perch, bream, rudd and eels are all in plentiful supply. Both lakes have relics of early settlement, and Lower Lough Erne, in particular, has many islands with pagan and early Christian monuments; the islands were used as stopping places in medieval times for pilgrims to Lough Derg. Devenish Island, which has a perfect round tower 80 feet high, is one of the most magical places in Ireland. A monastery was founded here in the sixth century by St Molaise, who was Columcille's mentor, and at its height taught fifteen hundred students. Nearby is White Island which has a ruined twelfth-century church. Lined up on the far wall of the building are seven impressive stone figures whose significance has never been resolved; one is a Sheila-na-Gig (see p. 130). On Boa Island are a two-faced Janus idol from pagan times and Lusty Man, a smaller idol with an outsized head and womanly arms which was originally sited on nearby Lustymore Island – hence the name.

I suggest you now turn north-eastwards, crossing from Fermanagh back to Tyrone, and make for the old O'Neill capital of Dungannon. A few miles north of Dungannon itself is Tullyhogue, a great circular enclosure on a wide-angled hilltop which was the inaugural seat of the O'Neills for some fifteen hundred years. South of Dungannon, almost on the Tyrone border with Armagh, is Benburb, site of Owen Roe O'Neill's superb victory over a Scots–Ulster–English army in 1646.

Head now for Armagh city, Ireland's primatial capital and seat of two archbishops of Armagh – Catholic and Protestant – who co-exist harmoniously. Although the Anglicans took over the see and old cathedral at the time of the Reformation, the bulk of Ireland's population does not recognize the claim,

regarding the Catholic primate as the true inheritor of St Patrick, who founded Ireland's first diocese here in the fifth century. Armagh, largely Georgian today, is among Ireland's most beautiful towns. It was ravaged several times by Vikings, though King Brian Boru, who was buried here in 1014, restored its prestige. With the Reformation, it was attacked by the Irish themselves more than once and became a desolate and squalid place. It remained so until the early eighteenth century when the Church of Ireland archbishop spent a fortune beautifying the town, building an episcopal palace, restoring the cathedral and, in 1793, founding the famous Armagh Observatory, which stands high on one of the city's several hills. Perched prominently on another hill is the twin-spired gothic-style Catholic cathedral, which was completed in 1873; despite its imposing exterior, the interior lacks distinction.

Roughly a mile west of the city lies Emhain Macha (Au-in Mawha), a great grassy knoll which Ptolemy marked on his map as Isamion, one of the few 'towns' of ancient Ireland. There is not much to see, alas, but to anyone familiar with the great Celtic literature of the Heroic Age, this is a hallowed place. Here King Conor and his Red Branch Knights held dominion over large parts of Ireland; here walked the great champion Cuchulainn and here, too, was acted out the tragedy of Deirdre of the Sorrows and the sons of Uisneach. It was here that a kind of Irish Punic War was launched against Queen Maeve of Connacht, which ended only when, with both Maeve and Cuchulainn dead, the Connachtmen overran the place in about AD 450, destroying the palace of King Conor and the headquarters of the Red Branch Knights. This is a site, if you know anything of Irish history, from which it is difficult to tear oneself away.

You should now thrust south-east to the border town of Newry, which is reputed to have been

Dunluce Castle, Co. Antrim, was built by the Norman Mandeville family, who later changed their name to the more Irish-sounding MacQuillan.

founded by Patrick himself. Swift wrote of it, 'High church, low steeple/Dirty streets, and proud people', but Newry, though a depressing town, is better than that. It occupies a strategic position between the plains of Louth and those of the North with the result that it has, to its detriment, been much fought over. Nothing can take away, however, from the grandeur of the Newry hills – Slieve Gullion (almost 2000 feet high) to the south-west, and the outliers of the Mournes to the east. It is now a magnet for citizens of the Republic who can buy a range of goods cheaper in Northern Ireland than at home. The road along the west side of Carlingford Lough, which is connected with Newry by the oldest canal in the British Isles, will take you round the Cooley Peninsula and into the Republic; if you wish to stay in Ulster take the road to Warrenpoint.

With its colourful esplanade and enormous square, Warrenpoint is the prelude to a superb coastal drive round the foothills of the legendary Mourne Mountains. In the shadow of their highest peak, Slieve Donard (2796 feet), is Newcastle, one of Northern Ireland's main seaside resorts. It is a neat, clean little place with the usual facilities for a none-too-sophisticated holiday and, whatever else is lacking, the great slopes of the Mournes sweeping down to the sea will inspire and delight the eye. They are a noble sight, fifteen miles long and eight wide, with no fewer than twelve beautifully rounded summits over 2000 feet high. Newcastle is a centre for exploring them, which is best done on foot, but whether you walk or drive, you will find their great granite masses, cliffs and moraines extremely rewarding. If you walk, make for the Hare's Gap, where you might be lucky and pick up precious or semi-precious stones – topaz, beryl, even emeralds – which have penetrated the granite.

Just outside Newcastle lies Tollymore Forest Park and, a mile or so further on, the unexpectedly well-

The Giant's Causeway, Co. Antrim. Legend has it that Finn MacCool built it as a causeway to the Scottish island of Staffa.

The Watergate, Enniskillen, rebuilt by the Scottish William Cole in 1609. It sits astride a ribbon of water connecting Lower and Upper Lough Erne.

laid-out market-town of Castlewellan, which is almost English in style. It too has a park, with exotic plants and a magnificent arboretum dating from 1740.

Rejoining the coastal road at Dundrum, you should not miss the ruins of a spectacular Norman castle, claimed in its day to be the most impenetrable in Ireland. It is said to have been built by John de Courcy who carved out a kingdom for himself here in the twelfth century. Continue along the coast to the picturesque fishing port of Ardglass which must once have been quite a splendid place. Jordan's Castle, a fine example of a Co. Down tower-house with an impressive complement of turrets, has been turned into a small museum. You have now reached what the Tourist Board have carefully labelled 'St Patrick's Country'. It was in 452 that Patrick, having been

A two-faced pagan idol on Boa island, Lough Erne.
Moss-covered tombstones and encircling hazel trees
emphasize the druidic nature of the place.

rebuffed in Co. Wexford, 'sailed up to Down'; having negotiated the narrow entrance to Strangford Lough ('the violent fjord' as the Vikings called it because four hundred million tons of water rush through the gap twice a day) he landed somewhere on the Lecale Peninsula. An Anglican church now marks the site of a barn where he preached his first sermon. According to the Book of Armagh, he was eventually buried in nearby Downpatrick 'on the great hill'. The site is now occupied by an Anglican cathedral but it was previously marked in turn by a sixth-century monastery, an Augustinian abbey, a Benedictine abbey and several earlier cathedral churches. A granite monolith near an old round tower in the cathedral grounds is said to mark the saint's grave. (John de Courcy claimed to have dug up the remains of Ireland's other two great saints, Columcille and Brigid, and interred them alongside Patrick – which may or may not be true.)

Strangford Lough itself, though much quieter than the rocky coast of Antrim, is one of Northern Ireland's scenic gems. Drumlins – small rounded hills formed by glacial action – which cover much of Co. Down, even march into the lough, creating small islands which are breeding grounds for wildlife, particularly seals. The immense, mirror-like expanse of water, framed by woodland sloping gently down to its shores, reflects a series of Norman castles set majestically against the skyline. At the upper end of the lough is the Nendrum monastic site dating from the fifth century. Just outside the small town of Strangford is Castleward (now National Trust) which was acquired and rebuilt by Bernard Ward, MP for Co. Down (later first Lord Bangor), in the 1760s. The approach shows a fine Palladian mansion, which was what Ward wanted, but the back of the house is Strawberry Hill Gothic in the fashion of the day, a fashion his wife Anne insisted on following. Inside the house this divergence of tastes is equally apparent: his reception rooms, at the front, are coolly classical and restrained; hers, at the back, are a riot of gothic vaulting and icing-sugar pendants.

You have the option now of taking a ferry from Strangford to Portaferry on the Ards Peninsula, or, if you have the time, following the west loughside road as far as Newtownards, doubling back down the sheltered east side and from Portaferry making your way along the pleasant coastal road to Belfast. Whichever route you choose, make sure you see Killyleagh, on the south-west shore, which has an extraordinary Loire-château-cum-Scottish-baronial-style monster of a castle, all cones, turrets and crenellations, which has been the home of the Hamiltons since the seventeenth century. One of the towers is actually Norman but the whole place was rebuilt in fairy-tale style in 1666.

The great sandy beaches at Newcastle, Co. Down, are backed by the Mourne Mountains. To the left rises Slieve Donard, the highest peak in the range at 2800 ft.

There is a stone at the castle commemorating Killyleagh's most famous son – Sir Hans Sloane, physician to George II – whose collection of fifty thousand books and three thousand five hundred manuscripts, as well as a cabinet of curiosities, formed the nucleus of the British Museum (he is also credited with being founder of Kew Gardens). The young Sloane educated himself in the castle's library before moving to London in 1712, where he is remembered in the names of Sloane Street, Hans Crescent, Sloane Square and a Circle Line underground station.

The few minutes' trip by ferry from Strangford to Portaferry is just enough to give you an idea of the beauty of this inland sea. Portaferry is an excellent place to eat, superb for oysters and other shellfish. The drive to Greyabbey, clinging close to the lough, is a pleasant one and the ruined Cistercian abbey is still worth seeing. In an idyllic setting, it was founded in 1193 by Affreca (daugher of the king of Man and later the wife of John de Courcy) and it is notable for showing the first signs of gothic style in a country which was still resolutely romanesque.

Continue along this lakeside road for a few miles to reach Mount Stewart and its superb gardens, former seat of the Marquis of Londonderry but now owned by the National Trust. The house itself, a largely eighteenth-century mansion, was once occupied by Lord Castlereagh, Pitt's Foreign Secretary; as one of the architects of the Act of Union which destroyed the Irish Parliament, he earned himself the opprobrium of nearly all Ireland and eventually took his own life. Internally, it is not a particularly splendid house and many of the upstairs rooms are gloomy (though it does contain twenty-two Empire chairs used at the Congress of Vienna – Prince de Tallyrand and the Duke of Wellington were among the delegates who used them). But of course the gardens are Mount Stewart's chief

The gardens at Mount Stewart, Co. Down, former seat of the Marquesses of Londonderry, benefit from the warming effect of the nearby Gulf Stream.

The waters of Strangford Lough, Co. Down, are alive with fish, seals and bird life. Its gentle shores are studded with the remains of ancient monasteries and castles.

delight. Laid out on a grand scale, they are mainly the work of Lady Londonderry, wife of the seventh marquis, who from 1920 onwards laboured to create something really magnificent. Planted with a fascinating collection of trees and shrubs from around the world, they include an Italian Garden, a Spanish Garden, a Sunken Garden, a Shamrock Garden and many more, plus a marvellous piece of topiary in the shape of an Irish harp.

If you prefer to follow the coast road, double back to Greyabbey and cut across the peninsula to Ballywalter. The drive northwards from here to Bangor is bucket-and-spade country, the pleasant but hardly dramatic coastline dotted with small, undistinguished little fishing villages. At Millisle you will see the Ballycopland windmill, the only working one in Northern

Ireland. Donaghadee is notable for its bracing sea air and its fine harbour, with a lighthouse designed by Sir John Rennie and David Logan who build the Eddystone light. It is the nearest Irish port to Britain, the crossing to Portpatrick in Galloway being only twenty-one miles. On calm days local boatmen used to row passengers to Scotland for £5, and it was common enough for members of the Presbyterian community to attend services in Scotland on a Sunday. Donaghadee has had more than its fair share of famous visitors: Boswell in 1769; Keats in 1818; Daniel Defoe and Wordsworth also came here, and Franz Liszt, a piano among his baggage, was stranded here for several days because of bad weather. The inn in the high street, which has been open for business since 1611, has a tradition – it is no more than that – that Peter the Great stayed there when he made a tour of Europe to learn Western technical and shipbuilding skills.

Today Bangor is the rather dull, nondescript 'premier' seaside resort of Northern Ireland, much of it as tawdry as you can imagine although it has delightful suburbs. A mere twelve miles from Belfast, it has largely become a dormitory for the city, and the thousands of seaside visitors who cram into it every summer come to enjoy its beaches rather than to recollect its ancient importance. Indeed, there is nothing left to remind them of its past glories. But it was in fact here, in 559, that St Comgall founded one of Ireland's most celebrated monasteries, which flourished for some eight hundred years. And it was from Bangor that some of the most eminent of the *peregrini* pilgrims departed on their stupendous journeys. The most famous of these was St Columbanus, who wandered all over Northern Europe founding schools and monasteries. Three of his foundations still exist, including one at Bobbio, near Milan. Sadly all that remains of great Bangor is the *Antiphonarium Benchoreense*, one of the oldest of Irish ecclesiastical manuscripts, now housed in the library there.

As we drive out of Bangor, along the shores of Belfast Lough, our odyssey round the strange, enigmatic land of Ireland is complete. One of the most beautiful countries on earth, it is also one of the most complex and contradictory. A land of myths and heroes, and monuments that might have been raised by men contemporaneous with those of Ur of the Chaldees, it has had a history of much savagery, poverty and despair. More Irish still live out of Ireland than in it, and the drain of emigration is perpetual. Yet when the gods smile on it, as they do on those soft Irish days which cannot be replicated in any other country, where else would one want to be?

Killyleagh Castle, Co. Down, a Scots-baronial style structure built in the seventeenth century. One of the towers is original Norman work.

Index